CATS AND OTHER IMMORTALS

CATS
AND OTHER IMMORTALS

Jean Overton Fuller

Bambi

FULLER D'ARCH SMITH
Steep House
6 Church Lane, Wymington
Rushden, Northamptonshire
NN10 9LW

ISBN No. 0-903394-98-7

Fuller d'Arch Smith Ltd has pleasure in acknowledging
the kind cooperation of Mandrake of Oxford

Photoset and printed by Stanley L. Hunt (Printers) Ltd, Midland Road, Rushden, Northamptonshire

CONTENTS

ILLUSTRATIONS

Drawings
Bambi as a Baby, on title page
Bambina, 14 January 1974, page 8

Oil-Paintings
(sizes of originals in inches; dates in some cases)

Plate 1 (facing page 10)
Memory of Whitfield Street, left to right: Tano with Cynthia and Bambina, Jean-Louis with Tiutté; behind them, the little oak-tree in its pot, 18 x 14
The Great Oak, Sherwood, 1972, 18 x 14
Excavation at Dawn, Sherwood, 1972, 18 x 14, exhibited at Chelsea Art Society, 1976
Jean-Louis Perret (top), 12 x 10
Tano Casiraghi, 12 x 10
Timothy d'Arch Smith, 1972, 14 x 10, exhibited at Bedford Art Society Jubilee Exhibition, 1979

Plate 2 (facing page 11)
Cynthia, portrait, 23 July 1975, 14 x 10, exhibited at Chelsea Art Society, 1975
Bambina on the Cabinet, one leg over, 30 October 1979, 18 x 14
Bambina frolicking on the lawn, 29 September 1979. 14 x 10
Cynthia in the Garden, on the stone slab (top right), 22 July 1976, 14 x 10
My Hens (my first painting of them), 29-30 August 1977, 18 x 14
Bambina Stretched on Carpet, 30 October 1979, 14 x 10

Plate 3 (facing page 26)
Bambina, portrait, 11-18 March 1987, 18 x 14, exhibited at Bedford Art Society Jubilee Exhibition, 1979
Bambina Yawning, February 1980, 18 x 14, exhibited at Chelsea Art Society, 1981
Bambina on her Second Birthday, in My Arms, Against Sunflowers, 18 x 14
Pansies, 17-18 May 1977, 8 x 6
Bambina on her Fifth Birthday, 14 x 10

Plate 4 (facing page 27)
Mother and Daughter, on patio, Bambina left, 28 October 1979, 18 x 14
Mother and Daughter, on sofa, Bambina left, 18 x 14
Mother and Daughter, back to back, Tiutté left, 18 x 14

The photograph on the back cover of Bambina looking at her picture was taken by the author in August 1988.

The photograph of the author on the inside flap was taken on 7 March 1991 by Shirley Warner.

TIUTTÉ

I T ALL BEGAN when three kittens appeared on the stairs, one tortoiseshell and white, one tabby, one ginger. The stairs were those of a newly converted block of "Luxury Flats" in Whitfield Street, between Tottenham Court Road and Fitzroy Square, a part of London known as North Soho. The kittens had been brought in by an Asian family, who had bought the flat under mine. They were well-to-do, owned a nearby Indian restaurant and ran a big car, but I wondered whether cats, like dogs, were unclean to them, since they did not take the kittens inside their flat. I had never known cats kept other than as pets, and it distressed me to see them always on the stairs — or rather, the stair, for they were always on the same one. The back door to the building was always open, and as winter came on the cold was perishing. Cats hate draughts. These were always in a freezing draught.

I would have liked to take them into my flat, but it was awkward as they belonged to the Asians and I hesitated to knock on their door. I consulted Mimi and Dave Clarke, a retired couple who had bought a flat on the top floor. I said I thought to buy a basket. Dave said, "No basket." People could trip over it. The stair-lights did not work as they should; Miss C was infirm and could break her leg. Mimi reminded me of a clause in our leases: nothing to be put outside the flats in the hall or on landings. She said, "My idea is that we should all keep the rules. Unless we keep the rules ourselves we shall lose the right to complain when others break them." Mimi had been headmistress of a school for sub-normal children.

What they said was true, but nobody but I was thinking from the point of view of the kittens. Their presence was, itself, a breach of the rules: no animal to be kept "except a small cage-bird". The Clarkes had not complained about the kittens, as probably they had been brought in to catch the mice. When the Clarkes had moved in, the place was overrun with cats; Dave had chased the cats out, which in retrospect he recognised as a mistake. He had telephoned the Town Hall and asked for the Rodent Officer but was told he was too busy. "It's because of the Dustmen's Strike. He comes only for rats."

A big rat had walked ahead of me up Whitfield Street, in daylight, and turned the corner into Grafton Way as neatly as any other road user. I like mice and rats, but not to find their droppings.

The Asians got the Rodent Officer to come to their flat every day for three weeks, but he did not eradicate the rodents. But I said to Mimi and Dave, "Those kittens couldn't catch mice. They're not big or strong enough. They need building up, and protection from the draught that comes in through that back door." It would not shut.

They were sad kittens. They never played. The ginger disappeared.

I hung a curtain over the outside of the door of my flat, picked up the two remaining kittens and placed them between the curtain and my door and in the recess placed a saucer of Complan.

Later, I opened the door and showed them they could come into my flat. I did not keep them in at night, as they belonged to the Asians below, and because it would have meant installing a tray, which might have smelled; but at least during the hours of daylight they had the benefit of central heating. Tentatively, I called them Pauline and Peter.

When Tim — Timothy d'Arch Smith, my partner in Fuller d'Arch Smith — came, I said, "Look," and set a saucer of Complan down.

He exclaimed, "They must be famished — to rush like that to a milk powder."

"It's got vitamins and minerals."

"But to rush to it like that."

One day, accidentally, I trod on the tabby. It fled, and I never saw it again, though I searched the streets. When I told Tim, he exclaimed, "Oh never tell my mother, that first there were three, then there were two and now there is only one."

She was a frightened, mistrustful kitten. Although she came in for Complan, she shrank if I attempted to stroke her. Yet once she lay all the afternoon on my bed. I studied her and came to know her markings. Tortoiseshell and white, she had black circles round her eyes, a small white blaze up her nose and on to the centre of her forehead. Her face was handsome really, only the little black markings beneath the corneas gave her an appearance as though she were crying. It still was not possible to fondle her.

Mimi, who called in, said, "If I put out my hand, she ducks."

"It's not your fault. I think she has had some bad experience." I added, regretfully, "She is not exactly the sort of cat it would be a joy to own."

Nevertheless, when I left the house she would sometimes accompany me to the corner of Grafton Way, or even round it, as far as the pillar-box. And when I had been out, she would, as I returned, sometimes come down the street to meet me.

I bought sketch-books and tried to draw her. The dated drawings start from November 1973. They were not very good, but I came to know the emplacement on her of every patch of black, white, red and cream. When she was not in my flat she sat in the hall, on the sole mat. Mimi said, "I never thought to see a child's primer illustrated: THE CAT SAT ON THE MAT."

But she was coming more to me. At first she had been afraid to step through the door. She was gaining a little confidence.

Each day when I opened the door of my flat to take in the milk and the letters, she was there, sitting with the letters and the milk; and I gave her breakfast.

Then her ways changed. At about half past five, she would sit in the hall below, facing the door of the flat opposite to that of the Asians. It was the only one let furnished, and had recently been taken by two boys, whom I heard talking in French.

It was on Saturday, 10 November, that as I stood on the step, one of them, the fair one, came up from the street and paused to get out his key. I said in French, the moon was full tonight, and he was delighted to hear his own language. His name was Jean-Louis Perret and he was French Swiss. His companion was Italian Swiss. "Won't you come in and have a tisane with us?" Tano (formally Graziano) Casiraghi was taller and darker. Behind one of the divans was a red silk square sporting a larger-than-life picture of Greta Garbo. She had been my mother's favourite actress and was mine. They were bank clerks and had been sent from a Swiss bank for the experience of working in a bank in the City of London. "When we go back, it will be to better positions," explained Tano. They opened a cupboard and showed me a row of tins of cat-food. "For Tiutté."

I had called her Pauline, or Little One, or Littlejohn to rhyme with it, but since the Swiss boys had given her a name so distinctive I adopted it.

I should not give the impression the Asians never fed her. Sometimes in the evenings they called, "Kitty, Kitty," and put out a plate of food. But once, when I saw her try to enter their flat, I saw a hand waft her away and the door shut in her face. A cat needs love.

Though I was generally vegetarian, at Christmas I had always shared a pheasant with my mother, till she died. Now it was with Tim and Tim's mother. This year it was at Tim's place and there were two pheasants. There was a lot left on the second and his mother insisted I should take it home with me. I did not feel I should eat it by myself and put it down for Tiutté. The little cat ate, and ate and ate, till she was so stuffed that she lay on her stomach with her four legs splayed round her. I was afraid she was going to die, but she recovered.

So we passed into 1974.

One day, when I thought she was inside my flat, I saw her sitting outside, but much larger. How had she made division of herself? Then I saw it was another cat. This was my first encounter with White Tom. He often came in after that, through the missing panel in the back door. Basically a white cat, he had a small tabby saddle and smaller tabby skull-cap, which descended over the top of his forehead to end just above the eyebrows so that it looked like a fringe; he had also a few black spots, on one side only. "To be discouraged," said Dave. He spoke of throwing something at him, and I was alarmed, but I never saw him do anything worse than say, "Grrr!" discouragingly.

He was not in my eyes a beautiful cat, but he was beautiful in the eyes of Tiutté. They followed him round, wide with admiration.

I doubted if the Asians had thought to have her spayed, but she was not my cat and I did not know what to do about it. In the summer, her belly grew round. Then, one evening, while I was at my typewriter, there was a knock on my door. Jean-Louis was there. "Tiutté's kittens are being born. Would you like to come down?"

Within their flat, one had arrived already. It was white, like its father, with patches of tan. While we watched, a second appeared, white with black patches, a third black with a few white hairs, and last, the smallest, a silver tabby, with white front and paws and "fringe" cut across like her father's.

Tiutté's eyes were shining. Delivered and proud, she was the very picture of radiant motherhood. A waif, she licked them clean and nice and gave them her teats, and I heard myself saying over and over again, "You are such a good mother!"

The boys' eyes, too, were shining; they had become beautiful as though they had witnessed the Virgin birth.

"The last is the most perfect," they said.

"Did you notice the time she was born?" I asked.

"It was a quarter to ten," said Tano. The date was 2 June.

The boys loved her, first for the symmetry of her markings, her daintiness, then, in the days that followed, because she was the first to walk, the quickest to learn everything, the most affectionate. Jean-Louis said, "It is something that was not, and which is – something new."

I saw that for him the whole mystery of creation was vested in the tiny, striped figure on his palm. He said, "It's our cat. We saw her born."

They would not tell the Asians Tiutté had had kittens in case they claimed them. They kept her and the kittens inside their own flat all the time. Tano told me he took the silver tabby into his bed every morning, and held her against his heart for half an hour before he had to get up.

Because she was so small and perfect, I called her Pearl. As soon as I had given her that name, I hoped it would not prove unlucky. Poets likened pearls to tears.

The white, first-born kitten remained the largest, but was slow. Jean-Louis took against him for this reason. I said he was stalwart and called him Lion. The black was also slow, and timid, we did not get to know her. I began to like the white one with black patches, one on one cheek, dividing the face after the manner of the harlequin. I called him or her Clown.

The boys wanted to keep Pearl until they had to go back to Switzerland, and then give her to me. She was very winning, and so was Clown, but two things made me reluctant. I did not want to have to enter a butcher's shop as I hated the sight and smell of carcasses, and even if I bought tins, there was the expense. Also, I did not want a sanitary tray in my flat. I told Jean-Louis I would take on her feeding if she came in and went out down the stairs to the street. He was horrified. "She must never go out."

I talked to Tim about it. He had a ginger brother and sister (the latter now deceased) and I remembered his attributing the problems with their health to his having to keep them within his flat all the time. "I think they are never completely healthy living indoors."

But now, when I consulted him, he said, "You have to keep them indoors."

"But when I was a child, in Beckenham, we had a cat and he used to go in and out."

"It must have been very quiet where you lived. If one had a house in the country one could keep a cat like that. In London, it's impossible."

We were in his flat, in St. John's Wood. He implored me not to have a cat. "It's something you take on, on an impulse, in a moment of generosity, which is a chain for years."

It was in such a moment that he had taken in the pair of gingers, to save them from being put down. "You can never go away without arranging for someone to come into your flat every day to feed them and change their tray. Unless you put them in kennels, which is expensive and makes them miserable."

Yet later in the evening, as he looked at Dizzy, curled on the rug, he said, with gloomy foreboding, "You may have to have a lot of little brothers and sisters."

"You are a saint," I said.

"I don't want to be — if there is any other solution." He got up and paced the room. "You have to be firm. You don't have to give reasons. All you have to say is, 'I don't want a cat.' "

The boys took it hard. "We would take her to Switzerland, but there is the quarantine." They had asked at the bank but none of their colleagues wanted a cat.

They would not consult the Asians, in case they had the kittens destroyed. After three weeks, they let Tiutté out, through their window. The Asians, seeing her again, after this long absence, said in mild surprise, "Hullo, Kitty."

They were never told she had had kittens.

I began ringing and writing to all my friends. I tried forty-nine people, including some I had not been in touch with for years. Everyone either had a dog, had a cat already or did not want a cat. I made trunk calls to Lancashire and Cheshire. . . . I opened the *Yellow Pages* and made telephone calls to thirteen pet-shops, asking, "Do you take kittens?" I had heard, "No," so often I could hardly believe it when Pets' Parlour answered, "Are they eating?" They would take them if they were between five and seven weeks and eating strongly. What colours were they? I told them. They liked the sound of Lion, "Because he has the patches of ginger. We shall find him the easiest to sell."

"But you'll take all of them?"

"Providing they are eating strongly. We've never had to let anyone down yet."

Lion began to lap Complan and milk, then eat. So did Clown, and the black one. Pearl did not take the food, but went back to her mother's teat.

One evening, at eleven, there was a knock at my door. The two boys were there, wide-eyed with distress. "Tiutté's milk-glands are swollen. She cried in pain. What must we do?"

I did not know, but went down to look. Tano, clasping her in his arms, said, "Her teats are hard. See, the glands beneath them are swollen." As he parted her fur to show me, she whimpered.

Tim gave me the address of his vet, Michael Lawson.

Would his surgery be open before office hours? If so, the boys could take her on their way to work. Otherwise, they would bring her up to me, and I would take her later, by taxi. They did not bring her, and afterwards told me that in the morning they had found her better.

They had two weeks Annual Leave and had booked a holiday in Italy. "If you will keep Pearl in your flat for the two weeks we are away, when we come back we will keep her for a year, until we have to go back to Switzerland."

"I will keep her for the two weeks if at the end of the year you can take her with you to Switzerland. In two weeks it will be too late to take her to Pets' Parlour, and in a year it will be difficult to find anyone to take her. She will love only you."

To tell the truth, keeping the kittens hidden within their flat was taking its toll of the boys. The smell had become strong, although they were scrupulous in changing the litter and used air-fresheners. "We have to buy two pints of milk a day. Not for us. Just for the cats." The kittens caught at their ornamental plants. "They go for that," said Tano, indicating the trailing purple leaves of the tradescantia. Their sleep was affected by Tiutté's demands to be let in and out during the night, and they began to look tired.

They took photographs of the kittens in every position. Then, on 13 July, they told me they had put all the kittens in a hold-all and taken then to Pets' Parlour. When they saw Pearl in the window, they wept.

"Was she eating?"

"No. The first in everything else. The last in that."

My heart sank. If she had not eaten at home, how would she amongst strangers?

It had been their last free day before they left for Italy, they explained. If I had known there was that problem, I would have kept Pearl in my flat till she was eating and taken her then.

We were all most unhappy.

I wanted to have Tiutté spayed. White Tom was already coming round again, and I could not face the nerve-wear of having to place a second litter of kittens. Even the boys, when they came back, agreed. "Once it was wonderful; a second time, it would be too much," said Tano.

How was I going to get her to the vet? To pack her into a container would be difficult and I did not wish to be seen by her lawful owners carrying her out. I should not give the impression my relations with them were bad. Tim and I had dined one evening at their restaurant. I had mentioned that my father had been an officer in the old (British) Indian Army, and was one day honoured in that one of their servants climbed the stairs to present to me a dish piled high with golden rice and things delicious, "Because it is the Muhurren." It was so I learnt they were Muslims. Whereas Mimi Clarke had a running quarrel with them about the dustbins, I was invited to come down and hear the famous singer and Indian orchestra they had engaged to entertain their guests. Seeing a pile of shoes at the door I removed mine and added them to it and took my place on the floor. I was the only non-Asian. Our host, pouring out, was exhorting everyone to drink "scotch!" which surprised me, as the Koran forbade spiritous liquors. Yet I still hesitated to raise the subject of Tiutté. Tano had bent to pat her one day and their child had said, "Now you want to wash yourself." Mimi, when I told her, said, "I'd have walloped him."

I rang Michael Lawson on 13 July. His secretary asked if I wished her inoculated at the same time. "Against feline infectious enteritis. If it's a question of only doing one thing Mr. Lawson would rather inoculate than spay." I agreed she should be inoculated as well as spayed, but saw the bill mounting. The appointment was for 17 July at 9.00 a.m.

I took Tiutté into my flat and tried, in advance, putting her in various boxes. She fought her way out of each, very much upset. Then the boys obtained an enormous box. They would keep her in their flat the night before and bring her up to me, in it, before 8.30 when they had to leave for the bank. In case the box failed, Tim lent me a cat-collar and lead.

On the evening before, Tiutté ran out. We all ran after her. Jean-Louis said, "Let Tano call her. She comes only to Tano." This was true. She had attached to Tano with devotion. He alone could pat her. After a time, she came to him. He picked her up and carried her into their flat. I set my alarm-clock for 7.30.

At 8.30 the boys came up, not to present Tiutté, in the box, but to say she had burst out of the box. "She is so strong!"

I went down to their flat to try to put Tim's collar and lead on her. She retreated and I was shocked to see she cowered from me. It was as if she knew there was some threat to her innards.

Just as we thought we had got her, she dashed out past Jean-Louis, through their door and out through the door at the back.

I went up to my flat. Through the window of my study I could see her. She was in a hole in the roof of the building opposite. The tip of her nose was showing. I rang Tim. I rang the vet, and said I would not be there, with cat, at 9.00. The appointment would be kept open for me until 11.00.

The boys had had to leave for their bank, but now John Norton arrived, a school-leaver at that moment working for Tim and me at the office. Tim had told him earlier that he should come and help me carry box containing cat to taxi, and had just telephoned him, "To make sure I did not fail to come and to tell me you might need help in catching the cat."

I took him into my study and showed him the roof with Tiutté's nose protruding. He went down, and, through the window, I watched him climb the wall, and then along the roof. He reached the hole and stretched his hand out. Then he retreated, and came back. She had been so fierce, he had been afraid she would scratch him if he attempted to pull her out.

I rang the vet again. After 11.00 the appointment would be cancelled.

I thought we should never see Tiutté again, but in the evening she came back.

The Swiss boys were leaving for Italy again on the morrow. Tano said, "We shall try again when we return."

By then, she would be pregnant again. White Tom was constant.

Since we had started to feed her, the Asians had ceased. Now I had to buy tins of cat-food. The least expensive smelled vile. Tim said, "It's because they contain lights." So I bought the better brands.

But what pained me was that Tiutté had lost her trust in me. I had to put the food outside my door, on the landing, as she was frightened to come into my flat. After some days, I could put it just inside the door, leaving it open, and she would enter and eat, providing I was not in sight. It was hard to believe she had once made her own way into my kitchen. All the ground that had been gained had been lost. She was, as she had been at the beginning, a frightened, mistrustful cat.

Yet sometimes she would meet my eyes, and I felt there was deep relationship. She had been shocked, yet communed with me.

White Tom reappeared in the hall. "Throw water at it," said Dave. I threw no water. It must be said, there were no longer any mice in the house.

The Swiss boys returned but they said no more about taking Tiutté to the vet. Her belly grew round again. They said, "We shall let her have them in the hall this time. Let those people see."

I dreamed of a second litter. One kitten was sky-blue and came towards me.

During September 1974 the Stock Exchange was falling. I could never live on the royalties from my books. I depended on the dividends from shares left to me. Food prices were rising. . . .

On 25 September the FT Index fell through the 200 barrier. I went to the office to talk to Tim. He was out. I left him a note in his typewriter saying I wondered if I should sell my flat and buy a house in the country, in case there was a crash as on Wall Street or hyper-inflation on the German scale.

Tiutté's belly had become so round and pendulous I expected her second litter that day. The boys and I had arranged a curtain over the table in the hall to give her privacy, and placed behind it a box. Several times I went down and looked, but there were no kittens.

At 9.00 in the evening I telephoned Martin Booth. Today I should call him the novelist, or the award-winning screen-writer, but though he was a poet and Tim and I had taken him on as Poetry Editor of Fuller d'Arch Smith, he still had a teaching job, in Rushden and had just bought a house in the North Bedfordshire village of Knotting. I asked, "Can I buy allotments near you?"

Allotments are allotted only to residents. But why don't you sell your flat and buy a house up here? Have Helen and me for neighbours."

While looking at houses they had seen one in the village of Wymington, just on the Bedfordshire side of the Northamptonshire border: fully detached, no front garden but very large garden at the back, oldish, two ground-floor reception-rooms, one of them large, four bedrooms "and two lavatories, one upstairs and one down." Warm-air central heating: £12,000 freehold.

I still could not get Tim, so I went up and knocked on the Clarkes' door. "Can I consult you about something? I bought my flat for £7,000. Do you think I could sell it now for £12,000?"

"Yes," said Dave. They were selling theirs, too. "Luxury flats! Fitzrovia!"

"Characterful," I suggested, and they both laughed.

I got Martin on the 'phone again. He said he would be free on Saturday, could meet me at Bedford and drive me to Wymington.

"I'm trying to meet a deadline for the book on SOE that Kimber commissioned from me. . . ."

"This has priority. The publisher can wait. The house may not."

In the morning, the morning of 26 September, while I was having my breakfast, Tim telephoned. He had found my note in his typewriter. "I think perhaps you should," he said. "Let us talk about it over a cup of coffee in the café on Percy Street."

He was worried about finance, too. The rates on our office had risen so high we would have to get rid of our lease. "Westminster has bankrupted other small businesses caught in the same trap." He would try to find a way out of it.

The house at Wymington could be registered at Companies House as the address of Fuller d'Arch Smith, I said, and if we were to get rid of the Westminster office I could store some part of our stock.

Tim gave me the number of an estate agent.

It must have been 12.30 to 1.00 when I returned to the flat. Tiutté was still walking about, though her belly was billowing out all round her. I telephoned the estate agent, and he said he would come to my flat to value it. This caused me to look around it, and at the staircase. On the landing below were the curtains I had hung to reduce the draught from the window. They could be brightened by washing, but were too high to reach. I brought out a chair, stood on it, and it turned over. My ankle was twisted so badly it hurt me to get back to my flat. I looked in the glass and saw that my lip was cut, though most of the blood seemed to be coming from my nose. I dialled the number of my doctor, Dr. Davies, a homeopath, and was answered by her senior partner, Dr. Blackie, the homeopathic physician to the Queen. I explained my predicament. "I can't come to see you, but I can tell you what homeopathic medicaments I have here and perhaps you would advise me which I should take." She did.

I medicated myself and laundered the curtains, which had come away in my falling grip. Then I saw that it was only two or three minutes to 5.30. The nearest shops would be closed before I could reach them to buy anything to eat. I remembered that there was on Cleveland Street one where I had bought greengroceries as late as 5.45. I walked to it as fast as my strained ankle would allow me, and brought back potatoes, tomatoes and carrots, and as I re-entered the house I looked again under the table in the hall.

In the box, Tiutté was surrounded by her kittens, a big white one, as before, a black one, a tabby one and, at the back, smallest of all, a tiny tortoiseshell and white. My sky-blue kitten.

I went up to my flat and turned on the TV. The news at 5.45 had just started. They were Sun Librans, of course, but to have been born at this hour of the afternoon must have had Aquarian Ascendants. I went down later to look again and there was one more, a second silver tabby, even smaller than the replica of their mother. With white front and paws, this last one looked like Pearl; and her Ascendant would be Pisces.

So, on the day my life changed, the joys of my heart were born.

BAMBINA AND CYNTHIA

I TOOK THE TRAIN on 28 September, and bought the house in Wymington. But the formalities were long. In Whitfield Street, Tiutté and her litter were still in the hall, in a cardboard box the boys had lined with something pink. One afternoon when I came in, it was gone. I thought they had all been murdered. Then I saw that it had been moved further back, into the darkness behind the stairs. Tiutté and her kittens were all in it. The boys came out of their room. They, too, had received a terrible fright. "All killed!" said Jean-Louis.

Later Dave explained, "I've moved them further back, so that if they're here to stay they're not the first thing everybody sees when they come in."

Mimi said, "They take £2,000 off the value of the flats."

"I'll go to Bourne & Hollingsworth's and buy a basket," I said, "I don't think anybody wanting to buy a flat would be put off by a basket with a cat and kittens."

Dave spent hours with a vacuum cleaner on the staircase and landings, but it did not pick up the cat-hairs.

To talk to the kittens, I crouched on the stairs and looked down into the well behind. Their eyes had opened now. Somewhere I had read that in choosing a kitten one should take the one that comes towards one. I had marked the tiny tortoiseshell and white, and it was she who, from the back, raised herself on her wobbly legs and staggered over the others to me.

I did not like to take her from her mother too early, but on 30 October I picked her up to take into my flat for the first time. As I did so, the tiny tabby and white, the last born, came towards me too, asking to be picked up. I took them both, and sat with them in my study. The tortoiseshell and white examined the bookcases, legs of table and stool, and the tabby and white jumped onto my lap and played with the typewriter keys. I knew that I had to take them both.

What was I going to call them? The tortoiseshell and white was exquisitely graceful, and leapt about, sure-footed as an ibex, delicate as a gazelle. I called her in my mind Gracilis, Antelope, but these were not personal names. Tano addressed her as Banbino, baby (masculine). I said, "She is a girl. It should be Bambina." This could be shortened to Bambi, the gazelle on the advertisements for champagne. She was like champagne.

The tabby and white was also a girl. I noticed that the tips of her ears were white, so that from behind, one saw the two white points sticking up above the darker back. I called her White Ears, then Whitaker, which rhymed with it. But the ears were not merely tipped but edged with white; the crescent put me in mind of that on the wings of the Cynthia moth I had hatched as a child. Her name was Cynthia.

Tim was the first to know. He called and I led him into the sitting-room and said, "This is Cynthia."

He saw on the couch the tiniest mortal curled. His mouth opened in a great smile, and he melted utterly as he repeated, "Cynthia."

Then Bambina rolled Cynthia over.

The Swiss boys noted how the second litter replicated the first. Jean-Louis said, "The big white one is like the big white one last time." The tan patches had been replaced by black, but the temperament was the same. So it was with the black, the

9

second largest but most timid. When would he see that Cynthia repeated Pearl?

It was Tano who said, looking at Cynthia, "We did not think much of this one at first. Now we think it is the best. It is like Pearl."

I knew they felt Pearl had come back to them, and they could be right. Excepting for the addition of the tabby without white, it was as if the whole first litter had died and come back to us. I felt that Bambina was Clown. Though there was the notable addition of tan, there was the same harlequin pattern in the markings; but black came down further on one side of the face than the other, while over her shoulders the black and tan rippled in diamonds. Like Clown, she was the cheerful one — bubbling over with friendliness and confidence.

What no one had yet told me was that the first born is always the biggest and strongest for it has worked its way to the head of the queue. The others follow in descending order of ability. The last two, which I had chosen, would be the most delicate.

Though I took them into my flat for part of each day, I returned them to Tiutté at night. Though Bambina learned to sip from a spoon, Tuitté was still giving them suck.

Miss C said she would take the white one. Miss C was now putting down food, which was generous for her means were slender, but she put down too much — plates piled high with shredded red stuff. It was hardly touched, and it smelled. Jean-Louis said, "It's dog food. Nobody likes it." I tried to tell Miss C that a cat's stomach occupies only part of a cat, but, she said, the piles of food went down. They were going down the boys' lavatory. What I did not then know, was that tinned dog-food, though cheaper than cat-food, because of the coarser meat, sometimes contains an ingredient poisonous to cats.

The smell in the hall grew worse. Discussions took place as to whether this was because the kittens peed, Miss C's dog lifted its leg or White Tom sprayed. It could have been all three of these things which blended with the aroma of curry from below to create the "house special". Tano had learned one English word which he frequently used, "Stink".

Dave put down a bottle of disinfectant. I put down a bottle of disinfectant. Yet though the boys were always cleaning the feeding vessels, the stink remained. The boys said, "It's our fault. The milk we put out is overturned and goes sour in the carpet." They went down on their hands and knees with a basin.

I did not want my kittens to grow up in a stink. The boys said, "We'll keep them at night and bring them to you in the morning." I lent them the key of my flat and they opened the door each morning before they went to work, and put the basket inside. When I got up, I found them each morning sitting up in the basket, their two faces pressed together like the faces in the flowers of pansies. Each had a white blaze up the nose on to the forehead, but whereas in Tiutté this was regular, in Bambina it was more on the left and in Cynthia more on the right. Their faces were like the two halves of one flower.

I would lift them from the basket and carry them into the kitchen, where I made them their first saucer of Complan. They would spring up on the formica top while I was mixing it and start lapping before I put it down for them. After that I would give them something more solid while I had my own breakfast. They remained in my flat all day even when I had to go out — I had bought a tray — and when I came in for tea they would both jump on my lap. Later the boys would come up, sometimes only to change and greet the kittens before they went to a cinema, or to an opera at Covent Garden for which they had saved up their pay, but before they went to bed they would claim them from me. One day they filled their fur with Imperial Leather talcum powder. I was not

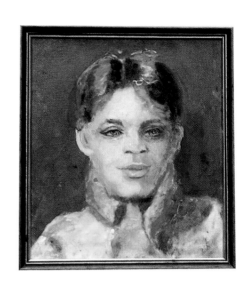

sure whether the kittens appreciated this, but Tano buried his face in them and said, "They smell good."

When I was alone with them, Bambina frisked all over the room, while Cynthia lay on my lap, her little paws on my breasts and her head between them. She was like a baby, soulful; yet it did occur to me that this might be because she was weakly, and therefore required extra nursing.

The boys had become absolutely enchanted with her. Tano held her up on his palm, cooing, "La gentilissima, la dolcissima gattina!" Aside, he added, "Bambina, a dire il vero, è un po' selvaggia." I was not supposed to understand that, but I had studied Italian years ago and knew it meant, "Bambina, to tell the truth, is a little wild." He would move to pick her up, but when he thought he had got her, she would dart away at some unexpected angle. Yet, to me, she came.

One day Tano, with Cynthia in his hands, said he found a lump beneath her abdomen. He said, "Can it be that she has something wrong? Cynthia!" He hoped it was only a piece of the umbilical cord.

I would be taking the kittens to the vet for their inoculations and would then consult him.

Miss C had taken the white kitten into her flat, and there remained only the black and the tabby without white, in the hall with Tiutté. Miss C was offended because when she put down a plate of food Tiutté scratched her. "She should love me. I feed her. If nobody is caring for her it would be best for her to be put down."

This sounded a new and sinister note. The Asians now said they would take her to the restaurant to join the red. It was so that I learned that the red or ginger was still alive. Neither I nor the boys liked the idea of Tiutté's being taken out of our care.

"She will never stay there," said Jean-Louis. "She will come back to us."

A few days later Jean-Louis heard the Asians' child saying something about a man's coming to give an injection. Swords were drawn over Tiutté and action had to be taken. Jean-Louis had thought of offering her to a girl at the bank, but said, "The difficulty is, she is not a nice cat." He corrected himself: "She is a nice cat, but she was badly treated so she fears and attacks everyone except us. If I were to give her to that girl, she would bite her."

I knew what I had to do. That night I telephoned Tim: "If I can get her to the vet to be spayed, I'll take her with me. I'll take all three to Wymington." I felt this as a prodigious undertaking.

The next morning when I came downstairs, Tiutté did a thing she had never done before. She came up and rubbed her body against my legs, and put her face up to mine. She had "heard" me on the telephone to Tim and knew she had an owner at last, she belonged to me.

Tim, when I told him, did not scoff. He said, "She knows."

From that moment Tiutté was reformed. Though never again so demonstrative as on that first morning when her joy overflowed, she was my cat. She came up to my flat, entered as she had not since she was a kitten, and went to her old feeding-place. It was not merely to see Bambina and Cynthia, for she came to me even when they were in the boys' flat. She had even withdrawn from Tano. He said to me one day, "It's all over between me and Tiutté. We are still friends but it is not as before."

I wanted to keep Tiutté in my flat all the time, but the two kittens no one had taken, the black and the elder tabby, could not be left in the hall by themselves. On 26 November I put them in a basket to take to Pets' Parlour. In the bus, a girl asked, "Is that a cat you have in that basket?"

"Yes. Do you want a cat?"

"Yes."

We got off the bus and walked to a place in Great Portland Street, where she worked. I opened the basket and she chose the black one.

"You wouldn't like the other one, too?"

"No. One will be a surprise for my husband. Two would be too much of a surprise."

I gave her a description of the siblings, parents and uncles, and my address, in case she had any problems. Then it was only the tabby, Frederick, I had to take to Pets' Parlour.

When I got back, I took Tiutté into my flat and made an appointment with the vet. On the last day before it, she was still suckling Bambi and Cynthia. "It is not possible!" exclaimed Tano. "Can Tiutté still have milk?"

"There is nothing there," said Jean-Louis. "It is habit."

The kittens bounded about Tiutté, and Tiutté bounded about with the kittens. Suddenly Jean-Louis exclaimed, delighted, "Did you ever see Tiutté like that?"

Tiutté was playing. When she was a kitten, she had never played. For the first time in her life, Tiutté had become a kitten.

Because she was so happy, it saddened me that her days of kittening were to be ended. I murmured to her, "You have been perfect, Tiutté, the perfect mother."

On 29 November, Tano took her in the basket, before they went to the bank, and handed her in at the vets. In the afternoon I called for her. She did not look so bad as I had feared. Michael Lawson said, "Keep the kittens away from her this evening." In the taxi I talked to her all the way back. "You have been the perfect mother. It is only that we could not have cared for as many as you could have given us, dearest. . . ."

A patch out of her fur, she sat quiet, but ate before bedtime. The boys said, "She looks better, sleeker, the colours brighter. . . ."

"They cleaned out her ears," I told them. "They didn't say if they also groomed her."

That night we cleaned the hall. Jean-Louis took up the cardboard which had been placed beneath the family and carried it to the dustbin. I produced a bottle of Jeyes Fluid. Tano sniffed it and recoiled: "It smells like public toilets!"

"It is used in them because it is strongly disinfectant."

He took it from me and went down on his hands and knees with a scrubbing-brush and a bowl. After that, the stink was no more.

As Bambina and Cynthia now lived in my flat, Tiutté slept that night with the boys. I would never let her into the hall again, and, the following evening, took her from the boys, into my flat, which she would not leave until I did, with the three of them. Bambina and Cynthia rushed beneath her to suck, and, though there must have been nothing in them, she gave them her teats. She was their mother. The operation had not destroyed the relationship. The emotions had not been cut.

We did not, however, let the kittens stay with her too long. That night Tiutté stayed with me, and the boys took the kittens. During the week I soothed her continually and the kittens were brought up to her for short periods.

Two days later I went again to the vet. In the taxi I had Tiutté in the new basket I had bought, to have her stitches out, and Bambina and Cynthia in a hold-all, their little noses sticking out like flowers. "My dears you are going to be made safe against infection."

Lawson gave the kittens their inoculations, and said, "Cynthia has a hernia." So that was what Tano had felt. It would require an operation, which could be performed at the same time as the spaying, at five months. "I'll do it from the front, so that there will be only a single incision. They have mites in their ears." He squeezed drops into them. "Two drops twice a day."

In the evening when the boys came up, Cynthia ran to Tano. During the week she had stayed with them she had transferred her devotion to him. I had difficulty in giving her the drops as she twisted so that they fell into her fur. Tano took her on his knee, but she flattened her ear back: "Now you don't have to do that. You don't like, but it is good for you."

White Tom called again. Tiutté, who had been so relaxed, now became wild. She wanted to join him. I let her out, and from the window of my study saw them facing one another on the wall. In the morning, when I opened the door to my flat, she was waiting to be let in.

I had been making paintings of places in Sherwood to which I made trips for research, and also filling sketch-books with studies of flowers in Regent's Park; now I filled sketch-books with attempts at Bambina and Cynthia, though they were always moving. I had learned to paint from my mother but in 1947-8 had studied in Paris at the Académie Julien. In the evening *Croquis* class, one would have to draw from the human nude whose pose changed first every ten minutes, then every five minutes and finally every two minutes. It was breathless work and quickened one at catching the main lines. Yet even with this practice behind me, sometimes I would have drawn but an ear before the kitten moved.

On 11 December, I took Bambina and Cynthia to have their inoculations. This time, Lawson said, "They're in beautiful condition."

They were glossy and shining, and in the taxi back I told them, "You have aristocracy of condition. You may not have pedigrees but I will *make* aristocrats of you."

This Christmas, of 1974, the boys went to their parents in Switzerland, and the kittens were reunited with Tiutté and me. Cynthia, I felt, missed Tano, but Bambina came forward to me. Bambina was *my* kitten.

Whilst I sat on the floor to make my Christmas cards, they sat on the paper catching at my brushes and — very persistently — drinking the painting-water. There was always a bowl of water for them but it did not compete for interest with that in which they saw my brushes dipped.

This year, Tim and his mother were coming to me, so I bought two pheasants. To keep them cool and away from my cats, I placed them on the inside window-sill of my study, beside the fern and the letters from the Foreign Office about the Déricourt file, and closed the study door. Later, I missed Bambina. I looked for her in the bedroom, kitchen, sitting-room, bathroom and at last in the study. Neither the fern nor the pheasants were on the window-sill. They were on the floor beneath my desk, on top of the letters from the Foreign Office, deep steeped in pheasant's blood. Bambina had removed most of the grease-proof wrapping. I spent the Eve washing the papers and returning the earth to the fern.

During our Christmas dinner, I had been expecting to have three little people dancing all round us, but Tim and his mother saw only the tips of their noses peeping from beneath the couch. They had not seen his mother before. As soon as Tim and his mother were gone, they came out and clamoured for pheasant.

As they grew, Bambina and Cynthia chased each other round and round the sitting-room, which I now perceived had three storeys. Using the tops of the sofa and chairs, the red Chinese scroll-table, black Chinese what-not and the oak sideboard, they could make continuous rounds without ever touching the floor. The third storey was constituted by the wall dividing the sitting-room from the kitchen, which did not reach the ceiling but bore ornaments. Bambina was the first of the kittens to be able to spring up on to it; then Cynthia managed it. Tiutté had never knocked things over; I removed the azurite and the cinnabar, but then the lamp-stand came crashing down and I do not know whose foot sent flying the silver statue of the Buddha. "The Blessed One will forgive you; you know not what you do."

My brass table attracted them. It was a very beautiful one my mother had brought back from India. I ranged the brass animals round it and polished it till it shone. Now it was always covered by paw-marks. Bambina, seeing her own reflection, was ceaselessly trying to reach the upside-down kitten below her, whose movements mimicked hers, whose nose came to meet her nose. Then, from the table, she saw herself yet more clearly in the long mirror, put her nose to the cold nose of the image and tried with her paws to part the glass from the wall, since her reason told her the other cat must be behind it. "It's yourself, Bambi!" Tiutté and Cynthia seemed at times to see their images but less certainly.

They kicked the telephone off its hook, and an address written by Tim on my notal pad disappeared – mysteriously till I noticed foot-marks on the erase bar.

I was concerned for the little oak-tree. My mother had picked it up as an acorn one day we sat at Kew, 2 August 1962. She had planted it in a hyacinth bowl, it had germinated and we had watched the cotylidons sprout, and the first pair of leaves on a tiny stem. After her death, I had brought it home in a taxi from her flat to mine. As it grew, I had transplanted it into a series of flower-pots. It was in a huge one now. The central-heating had brought it into bud too early. I had stood it on the scroll-table to get the light but now I feared the mischief of the kittens, and lifted it into the bedroom. My best sable paint-brush – they cost several pounds – had its hairs chewed off. One had to love them very much to bear it. My brushes joined the oak-tree in my bedroom, closed to cats. The light in the flat was far too little, and striving for it the leaves of the oak-tree grew far too large. I longed to get out to the country.

It was Cynthia who was most interested in my yoga. I had two days after their birth achieved my first headstand unaided. In all the poses, Cynthia would jump onto whichever part of my anatomy was uppermost. She was returning her affection to me, but when the boys came back she ran to Tano as though she was his cat. "It is something you cannot understand," said Jean-Louis. "Magnetism. Some people have it in other connections. He has it for cats. When I took him to my home, my cat jumped on his knee."

I said, "If you could take her with you when you go I would give Cynthia to you. Otherwise all three should stay with me." The boys came up when they could. Cynthia jumped distractedly from my knee to Tano's and back again, repeatedly. We had confused her emotional pattern. Yet with Bambina there was no confusion. Bambina was wholly my kitten.

In January, 1975, I had to fly to Paris for a few days. It was in connection with one of my books on SOE and was rather a worrying trip. I lent a spare key of my flat to the boys, to feed the cats. Then at last I was back. All three cats were on the couch. Bambina leapt into my arms.

CLEO

I WAS WALKING down Grafton Way when I saw, sticking up above the area steps of a house on the other side, the head and shoulders of a brown cat. I half passed it, when the thought came to me, "Cats aren't brown. Cats are white, black, blue, tabby, ginger or tortoiseshell. Not brown." A rabbit or hare? I crossed, to look at it better. It was the brindled brown of rabbit or hare, but it was a cat. It had deep amber eyes. It looked neglected, and it miaowed.

Another woman had come up. I said, "That looks forlorn."

She said, "That's a valuable cat. Burmese."

I did not think it was Burmese; yet it was one of the rare, non-European breeds. I said, "What do you think we should do? Should we take it to the police?"

The cat wanted to get into the house. Yet the windows were, on the ground floor, boarded up, and on the floors above, broken; the glass filthy. I supposed the house scheduled for demolition. Then the front-door opened and a man in shirt-sleeves let a child out. People lived in that house – probably squatters. I asked, "Is this your cat?"

"She has kittens upstairs," he said, evading the question. He let her in, but as a thing of no account.

I went home, looked in my manual on cats, and recognised what I had seen: Abyssinian.

When I thought of my own little no-bred cats, so cared for and cosseted, and that poor thoroughbred so neglected, I could not bear it. I wrote a letter to The Occupier about: "your brown cat. You do not seem to want her very much and I should love to have her."

I hesitated for a moment in case it should upset my own. Then I pushed it through the letterbox of that house. It was Thursday, 23 January, 1975.

On Sunday the 26th, my door-bell rang and a woman's voice said through the entryphone, "You want our cat. I've brought her."

A bedraggled girl had the cat in her arms. "She is a thoroughbred Abyssinian. She belongs to nobody," she said. Her accent was foreign. The cat had belonged to a woman who had lived in that house and had "papers concerning her". The woman had gone to Cornwall, leaving the cat, or perhaps had given her to a boy, who had also left. "She has diarrhoea."

"What are the kittens like?"

"Some were like her. Some were white."

I remembered White Tom lived in Grafton Way. The girl said homes had been found for all of the kittens but one. I gave her the address of Pets' Parlour.

I took the cat from the girl's arms and carried her into my sitting-room. Bambina did not instantly fly away and I had a moment's hope all would be well. But just as the girl was saying, "I'm glad to be leaving her with somebody who understands cats, has cats already . . ." I saw mine were fleeing in all directions. I reassured a cowering Tiutté, "You have nothing to fear from Cleopatra. You were my first cat. You will never be loved less."

I called the newcomer Cleopatra because I saw in her lines something of the Egyptian temple cat. I asked the girl to try to obtain her pedigree from the woman in Cornwall. "Or the address of the breeder, who might issue a duplicate."

"She must have been given the cat. She was not the sort of person who would have bought a cat from a breeder."

I asked the girl her name. She wrote down MARLISE and said she was Swiss.

When Marlise had gone, I sat Cleopatra in a basin of warm water. Although mine had been inoculated, I felt I was taking a risk in bringing in a cat from the street who was filthy. It was drastic treatment for a timid stranger. She struggled, but weakly, making far less protest than I had expected. I did not use detergent or soap in case it irritated her skin, but I rubbed the water into her fur, leaving only her head out, and changed the water a number of times, for loose hairs and fleas were floating out. The fleas drowned and I poured them down the lavatory. My fingers distinguished her ribs and the knuckles on her spine. Her sides were caverns.

At last I felt she was clean, towelled her and set her in front of the glowing bar of the infra-red fire. I saw that when one parted her fur, the hairs were apricot at the base up to about three quarters of their length, after which each one was separately banded with dark brown or black and then finally tipped with cream. The overall effect was tawny, though the apparent colour changed with the amount of inner fur exposed. Her underneath was apricot, as were her small feet, and there was a seal-dark stripe from just above the eyes, over the crown of her head and down the length of her spine to the tip of her tail. I brushed her and combed her in front of the fire, and she began to lick my hand.

I made her a saucer of Complan and she lapped it. I gave her a massive dose of homeopathic Sulphur 200 X and a tablet of vitamin C. There was continual growling from my cats, and I had to scoop up her yellow pools.

When I had got her reasonably respectable, I wrote a note to the Swiss boys. "When you come in, come up."

Soon afterwards they were at my door. I brought them in and said, "Look!"

"It's like a puma!" gasped Tano. He noticed the way she held herself, with her head high and her breast curving outward in a proud arch. "It's like a peacock."

I said, "Tiutté has gone down a hole."

"A hole? Where?"

"You cannot see it. If you kneel in front of the kitchen sink and stretch your hand behind it and upwards, you will find that behind where the pipe joins the basin there is a hole. Tiutté is down it."

Tano got down in front of the sink, examined the boards behind it and said, "It is not possible to reach her. There is a second hole, beneath the floor. She has gone down that. Suppose she cannot get out?"

"She got in; so she must be able to get out."

"But suppose it is one-way only, and she is trapped?"

They thought we should remove the wooden panelling, and I handed them my bread-saw. With this they removed a part of it and laid bare the bricks and entrance to the lower hole. But Tiutté was too far down to be seized.

We had lost count of the hours, and the boys said, "We must be at the bank in the morning. We must go to bed."

I collapsed on the sofa exhausted. It came to me that Tiutté might have felt pursued by my thoughts and would cease to feel so if we forgot her; but I was so nearly asleep that I was surprised by the flicker of an ear. Tuitté walked out into the room and growled at Cleopatra. I blocked the hole with the only things I could find, bottles of Silver Dip, then I went to bed.

In the morning, when I returned to the sitting-room there was nobody to be seen. No two little faces like the twin halves of one flower rose to greet me. Cleopatra was on a chair, but Bambina and Cynthia were uncomfortably perched on the tray of knives and forks in the furthest corner of the kitchen, bleakly unhappy. Tiutté had taken refuge on top of the high cupboard.

I would never have caused so much distress to my own dear cats. They were petrified. I made Complan, but Bambina and Cynthia did not leap on to the formica top to lap while I was stirring it. I had to pick them up and place them there.

Cleopatra came down from her chair to lap a saucer of Complan, but Tiutté would not come down from her high perch and I had to climb to put it up for her. Below, were yellow pools. I mopped them up and spread newspaper. When at last I sat down, exhausted, for my breakfast, Cleopatra jumped on to my lap and pushed her nose under my chin. This was an endearment, but her breath smelt putrid and it was difficult not to recoil. I telephoned Lawson and he gave me an appointment for that afternoon.

He said, "She has milk in her teats. There must be kittens somewhere."

"Homes have been found for them."

"Then it will dry up." He pointed to segments of tapeworm which adhered to her. He could treat her for that. Then he retreated exclaiming, "Oh my dear, she's full of fleas."

"I thought I had washed them all out."

"I just saw one." He showered her with flea-powder and went through her coat with a fine comb."

"I had better put flea-powder on Tiutté and her kittens, to protect them," I said.

"Yes, cover everybody with flea-powder."

I told him my cats had reacted against her. "This one is the aggressor," he said. "This is an entire cat. If there's a fight, don't try to separate them. You'll get mauled. Throw water on them." Then he said, "I've never known a girl called Cleopatra. I'll call her Cleo. I shall want to see her again in a week."

He wanted me to have her spayed, but it seemed a pity to deprive her of the chance of having beautiful kittens. When she was restored, I could have her mated with an Abyssinian cat.

It would be of no use, he said. Unless her pedigree was obtained, her kittens would be non-pedigree, could not be shown and he doubted if, even at reduced price, people would buy them. "It's a question of identification," he said.

When I got back, I found Cynthia and Bambina still huddled on the knives and forks. I dusted them with flea-powder. "I'm sorry to have to do this to you, my very dears."

Tiutté was still on her high perch, but came down from it. I was sorry to have to take the opportunity to dust her, too, with flea-powder, which sent her flying back to it.

I wrote to the General Secretary of the Governing Council of the Cat Fancy, for I felt I should report that Cleo was with me in case she had been lost by some owner who knew her value.

Then I walked to Foyles and bought a book on Abyssinian cats. In this, I found the address of a Mrs. I. Earnshaw, who was President of the Abyssinian Cat Club. I wrote to her too.

The book referred to a belief that the Abyssinian descended from the sacred cat of ancient Egypt. A cat had been brought from Abyssinia in 1868, but the authors, Alison Ashford and Grace Pond, thought the breed, as we knew it, the triumph of a small group of English breeders dedicated to the idea of recreating it.

"But how does a cat like that come to be in Grafton Way?"

Mimi, who had come down to look, suggested, "Perhaps she belonged to someone who died." The people who went into a house where there had been a death might not notice a little animal slipping out.

During the whole of the rest of the day, Tiutté growled. In the evening, however, she came down from her high perch and walked about the floor, though still growling.

Then something happened I would not have believed. Bambina was lying on the television set. Tiutté jumped on to the window-sill behind her and struck at her with her paw. The attack was unprovoked. I hoped it was a freak action, never to be repeated, but later she went for Cynthia, and then for Bambina again. Tiutté had turned against her kittens.

Although I knew that in nature mother cats withdrew from their kittens when they were old enough to feed, Tiutté's affection for Bambina and Cynthia had been sustained for so long, I felt that it was Cleo who upset her. Cleo, an adult cat, was too dangerous to attack, so the kittens, being smaller, received her ill-humour by transference.

"Come to me, my dears," I said to Bambina and Cynthia. "Your mother is upset and not herself at the present time. I am the mother who will never reject you."

So I prolonged their kittenhood, taking them into my arms.

On Wednesday, 29th, Tim came, and saw Cleo. He could not immediately see Tiutté. She was up on her high perch, growling.

I opened a tin of cat-food on to a plate on the floor. Cleo came to it first, then Cynthia, then Bambi. Tiutté saw, peered down at the food but restricted her movement to craning her neck and growling. Tim said, with gentle raillery, "You are silly."

"It's awful," I said. "The only two who still associate are Cynthia and Bambina. They keep together, everywhere. Bambina is the best behaved towards Cleo."

"She may be the best, but she is not faultless," said Tim. At that moment Bambina was growling at Cleo, though less volcanically than Tiutté, or even Cynthia.

I went out for something and came back. Tim said, "When you leave the room, there is a general displacement; and again when you return. They all love you."

Bambina and Cynthia now swarmed over me all the time. I was Mother Cat.

Then something else happened. One morning at breakfast. Cynthia was on my knee when Cleo approached. Timidly she crouched as if to spring on to my lap. I said, "Come," and she sprang. Cynthia struck her with her paw. Cynthia was jealous.

Cleo knew she was new here and always gave way, even to the kittens. Attacked, she never did more than stand her ground. Because of her internal condition I bought her raw minced beef. As it was expensive, I meant her to have it all, I set it down in the passage and took her out of the sitting-room into the passage. She was frightened at being excluded from the sitting-room. It was the haven to which she had been brought, and she feared only to find herself outside it again. She ate the meat, but with one eye on the door of the sitting-room, to which she hastened to return.

By Thursday, Tiutté was growling less. She walked about in a more natural way, less hunched. She still attacked Bambina and Cynthia, yet it was better than the frozen immobility in which she had crouched on the ledge. She even curved her body to my hand for patting.

On Friday morning when I opened the sitting-room door, Bambina and Cynthia were perched on the nearest corner of the couch to greet me, as before, Cleo stood on the floor just behind them. They almost formed a group.

On Saturday morning the kittens and Cleo were stationed as before, and Tiutté was under the couch, just visible. Cleo had almost been accepted.

Her diarrhoea had stopped and she had learned to use the tray. As soon as she did so, Tiutté, Bambina and Cynthia went elsewhere, so I had to buy a second tray.

Tiutté developed a desire to go out. Perhaps she wished to meet White Tom again, but I feared that if I let her go out while the flat was unpleasant to her from the presence of Cleo, she might not come back. She was regaining courage. Suddenly she walked up to the chair on which Cleo was sitting and slashed at her with a paw. Cleo leaped down and took a retaliatory swipe at Cynthia. It was the second time I had seen transference. The antagonists were too nearly of a size to risk conflict and struck the kittens instead of each other. Krishnamurti said once, "If a man speaks angrily to you . . . probably someone or something else has made him angry." I wished I could explain that to the kittens.

On 4 February I took Cleo back to Lawson. He expressed himself pleased by her improvement, but warned me again against cat-fights.

"The worst is over," I said. "There hasn't been an actual fight, so there won't be now."

"Don't be too sure. I shall want to see her again in three weeks. She will then be your cat."

I had until now been careful not to caress Cleo too much in case it made the others jealous. But that night, in the kitchen chair, as she was asking for affection, I patted her until the joy thrilled through her. Suddenly there were growls from the sitting-room. "Tiutté cannot see from there that I am stroking Cleo." Yet when I stopped, the growling stopped, and when I started again so did the growling. Then Tiutté came walking round the partition wall to transfix Cleo with her eyes, and Cleo flew at her, chasing her back to the sitting-room. I saw the pattern now. "The cat on my lap is the one with the position of rectitude and can dismiss the other."

Krishnamurti asks if one can have "the flame without the smoke" of love. With these, there is a lot of the smoke, yet the flame is not absent. There could not be so much smoke, unless there were the germinal flame.

Tiutté leaped on to the dividing wall and growled down. I talked to them both. "It is hard for you. You both have suffered, but you both are here with me to stay."

Cynthia came round the dividing wall. Cleo flew at her, chasing her back, then returned to my lap. Had I been wise to take Cleo on my knee? Till now, she had been meek. Established on my knee she had become aggressive. I set her down gently, and went to Tiutté, but she jumped on to her high ledge and sulked. She would never have permitted such petting as Cleo needed and joyed in, but to see Cleo receiving it was more than she could bear.

Krishnamurti takes jealousy and possessiveness as arising from thought, domination by thought. How, then, is it so strong in cats? It seems almost a primary emotion, love's first manifestation.

Cynthia let me take her in my arms again before I went to bed, and I left her reassured.

On the following evening, when the boys came up, we said it was strange that Cleo, an aristocrat, had been neglected, but Tiutté's kittens pampered from birth. "They are *bâtards de luxe!*" exclaimed Jean-Louis.

Tano rebuked him for saying such a sophisticated thing about such innocent little beings.

Jean-Louis had asked me to paint his portrait, and while I was busy with the oils, Tano said to me, "Tiutté licked Cynthia." I had despaired of her ever taking either of her kittens to her again. "It was only a quick lick," said Tano, "but it is the beginning of the return to normal."

But on Saturday I heard renewed growling. Cleo had taken the high ledge, hitherto sat on only by Tiutté. Tiutté crouched on the lower part of the dividing wall, snarling up at her. For the first time, I filled a basin with water and stood ready to throw it at the combatants, but Tiutté turned away and jumped down on to the scroll-table, where she hunched unhappily. Cleopatra was queen of the castle.

I felt sorry for Tiutté. It was true that Cleo had never growled, but in taking the high seat she had usurped, provoked. Later, as Tiutté was crossing the floor, Cleo ran after her, chasing her under the sofa. Cleo had become the aggressor. I tried to soothe Tiutté, but Tiutté, avenging her humiliation, flew in a blind fury at Cynthia.

Yet Sunday was quiet. No one assumed the high seat.

I knocked on the door of the derelict house in Grafton Way, and a man opened the door. I asked for Marlise and was admitted. There was no carpeting and the boards of the room in which she lived were bare. There was no bed; there were no chairs; just some cushions and cloths on the floor. I asked by what name the cat had been called.

"Bramble."

Have you been able to get in touch with the woman who went to Cornwall?"

"It's complicated," she said. "She was given the cat by a man who used to be here."

"What was his name?"

She had forgotten, but knew where to find him.

"Could you ask him for the pedigree or name of the breeder?"

"I am afraid he might ask for the cat back. He has not enquired about her in six months, but if I asked him about the pedigree he might ask for the cat back."

I ought to have taken this hint, confirmed by some male squatters. Instead, I pressed, "The vet says she will soon be in season. Then she will have to be either spayed or mated. Without pedigree, it will be hard to find homes for the kittens, yet it seems a pity to prevent such a rare and beautiful cat from having any."

"What do you want me to do?"

I told her the vet told me that in another three weeks she would be my cat. I had thought he meant in law, my having then cared for her for a month, and said, "After that, it would be safe to go to the man."

From the Governing Council of the Cat Fancy I had received a letter saying no loss of any Abyssinian cat had been reported to them.

Now I received a letter from the President of the Abyssinian Cat Club:

Dear Miss Fuller,
. . . What a blessing you took this poor little cat in and have looked after it — I would very much like to come and see you and the cat . . . this woman may have been given this cat and not wanted it and just left it. These people make me sick. I cannot tell you how grateful I am to you for taking the cat in.
                                                              I. P. Earnshaw

I telephoned to her and she said she would come to London before I left for the country.

Jean-Louis had suggested I write everything down, whilst my memory was fresh, and though I was trying to get on with my biography of Bacon I took time off to do this. I had reached this point in the narrative when, entering the sitting-room, I saw Tiutté, Bambina and Cynthia on the sofa together and Cleo on the floor close beside them. Harmony had been achieved. Should I end it here, "The room was at peace." Or perhaps, with the move to the country.

The formalities concerning the purchase of the house in Wymington and sale of my London flat were taking a long time. In the end, it was the Asian family below who offered me the best price for the flat. The restaurateur of the scotch came up to talk business, and, as he sat on the sofa, he saw Tiutté, with Bambina and Cynthia. A flicker of recognition passed over his face – a minor mystery must have been solved for him – but apart from a slight "Oh!" he did not pause in what he had come to say about the money.

I felt the spaying of Bambina and Cynthia even more keenly than Tiutté's. The appointment was for 21 February. The evening before, they were playing so happily, so trim of figure, so bright and bonny, and in the morning so sweet and confiding, it was terrible to have to put them in the basket knowing that when I brought them home they would have suffered surgery. I talked to them all the way in the taxi. "You won't have kittens, dears, but you won't be pulled down in health by bearing them. Your mother loved having you, yet she was terribly weakened and lost a lot of hairs. . . . Perhaps you will develop special qualities. . . ."

I left them with the receptionist and came back for them in the afternoon. "Are they all right?"

"Cynthia is a little wet. She spent a penny coming round."

I took them back in a taxi, crooning to them, "Poor little dears." In my flat, I opened the basket and they stepped out slowly and quietly. Cynthia at once used her tray, and though she could only move so slowly turned three times round as she should. "You have such good manners. Even suffering, you do not forget them." I wanted to say, "You are perfect," but did not, in case it should prove unlucky. "A little cat without a fault."

Cynthia was the one who had had the gravest surgery, for the hernia, as well, had had to be operated. Bambina, though quiet, looked less affected.

In the morning, when I got up and went into the sitting-room, they were both on the corner of the couch nearest the door, as usual, to greet me. They had cheered; and I cheered.

It was several days before either the boys or I dared to feel Cynthia, but when we did, that improper lump on her underneath was no more.

On Friday, 26 February, my bell rang. It was Marlise. She was carrying a small piece of paper and said, "I have written down for you the name, address and telephone number of this man."

I realised a month had passed. She had remembered. But in the meantime I had checked with Lawson; he had meant only that by this time Cleo would have settled down with me; it had no legal significance.

Marlise did not immediately give me the paper. She should first tell me about this man. "He's crazy, irrational. I'm frightened of him." If I got in touch with him, she would prefer me not to say it was she who had brought me the cat. "You could say you talked with a lot of people in the house and they all agreed you should have the cat."

"In what way is this man crazy?"

"Just mad. He does mad things."

"Can you give me an example?"

"He had a difference with one of the other squatters, and, to annoy them, arrived in the night with a big drum and beat it all through the night in the hall and on the stairs." She warned me again that asking for the pedigree might cause him to ask for the return of the cat, but said, "I've thought what you can do about that. You can offer him the first kitten."

"I don't think anybody who abandoned a cat is fit to have a kitten."

"You could offer it and then forget about it."

That was not quite my style. Wondering about her, I said, "It must be terrible living in that house."

"It is warm," she said defensively. "But it's very uncertain." There was no way to fasten the doors on any of the rooms, and unless they stayed in, other people might enter, throw their things out and squat in their places. "Every time one goes out, one knows what one could find when one returns. . . ."

After she had gone, I went down and talked to the boys. "Should I telephone to this man, or leave it?"

"It would be a pity to have someone come and take the cat away," said Jean-Louis.

I kept balancing. On 27 February, cautiously, I made my big mistake. I rang the number and asked, "Are you Mr. — ?"

"Speaking, but I don't use that name any longer. I now use the name — ."

"I have come into the possession of a cat which I understand used a long time ago to belong to you. The woman to whom you gave her abandoned her."

"Oh! She was supposed to be very fond of her."

"Do you still have the pedigree or could you obtain a duplicate?"

"I don't know if she ever had a pedigree."

"How did you obtain her?"

"I was given her, together with her sister, by a man for whom I worked at one time. I was surprised at his giving me two such beautiful cats." The sister disappeared. Bramble had two kittens. He did not want three cats, so he kept one kitten and gave the other and Bramble to the woman.

So Cleo had had two litters, the first consisting of only two kittens (one of which must have disappeared) before having the litter in Grafton Way by White Tom. I asked, "What was the name of the man by whom you were given the cats?"

"I can't remember. He lived in Barnes. If his name comes back to me I'll let you know. Where can I get in touch with you?"

This was a dangerous moment. I said I was leaving London and could give him only the telephone number of my office.

"I'd like to see Bramble again. Perhaps we could meet and let her and her kitten rub noses."

This was a friendly suggestion, to which I would naturally have agreed, but because of Marlise's warning I made some excuse to leave the phone.

Immediately afterwards I went to the house in Grafton Way. I found Marlise, and with her the young man who seemed to be her boy-friend; then another came in, and another. There were introductions all round, by Christian names. I told them about the telephone conversation I had had with the man. "He was beginning to get almost sentimental about the cat by the end."

"That's it," said the boy-friend. "He has not asked about her since he left the house. It's only because somebody else is interested."

"What is he by profession?"

"A furniture remover. Or did jobs for one."

"So we want a furniture remover in Barnes."

"He did jobs for several people. It would not be possible to trace."

At least, I thought, I had done my best to establish Cleo's provenance, and could forget it.

On 17 March, while Cleo was on my knee, Cynthia jumped on to it. Though they faced different ways, their backs touched. The Swiss boys were up, and Tano and I exchanged glances. A milestone had been passed.

Only Tiutté still cowered under the sofa. Her personality seemed to have become squashed. Jean-Louis, shocked, said, "She has forgotten Tano. I think she will never recover."

I would not admit the word "never". I talked to her. "You are my original 'little one' whom I found on the stair. I did not mean to bring in a usurper. Come out and be yourself." Yet with the coming of Cleopatra the life seemed to have gone out of her. Nevertheless, her growling was growing less. I said to her, "The red-letter day will be when *you* go through a whole day without growling."

24 March was a red-letter day in two senses. The contract arrived concerning the Wymington house and Tiutté passed the whole of it without growling.

On the following day, 25 March, Tim told me a woman had rung the office and asked for me to ring her back. The name she had left was unknown to me, and I was unsuspecting when in the evening I rang her number. She said she had had an Abyssinian cat called Bramble, whom she had left with a woman called Elizabeth. "Elizabeth had disappeared."

Elizabeth, then, must be the woman who had left for Cornwall. Who, then, was this woman? She had been given the office number by the man.

The woman said, "I've been trying everywhere to find what happened to Bramble. I want her back."

I felt shivery. This woman knew that the cat had been left at Grafton Way and need only have gone there to find her.

I said, "She was in a dreadful condition when I found her. Would you look after her properly?"

"Yes."

Playing for time in which to think, I asked if she could reimburse me the vet's fees. "Yes."

It was not what I wanted to hear. I parried, "She's still being treated for tape-worm and round-worm."

"I am a trained animal nurse."

I had never heard of such a thing and doubted it.

She said, "I should like to see Bramble. When can I come and see her?"

I said I was feverish, which was true, and would rather not continue the conversation now, and hung up.

Then I made a trunk-call to Mrs. Earnshaw. She said, "Wait a minute, while I consult my register. When she came back to the phone, she said that neither the name of the man nor the name of the woman was in her register. "Neither is the owner of an Abyssinian cat." Every Abyssinian cat was a registered individual, it had a registered name, date of birth and parentage, a registered owner and its own individual registration number. It was like a motor car; its number linked it to its registered owner, who could be traced. Every change of ownership was registered, and the register was with her. There were under two hundred of these cats altogether and the people who had to do with them were mostly known to each other. There was no registered breeder or owner in Barnes, or, indeed, anywhere in the London area, "If this cat is Abyssinian, these people have never been her owners. If they have ever been her owners, she is not Abyssinian, and has no pecuniary value." Apart from being a breeder of Abyssinians, Mrs. Earnshaw ran the Newbury Branch of the Cats' Protection League, which cared for strays.

The welfare of the cat should be placed first, she said. I should not hand it over to these people or make any move until the cat had been seen by her. She hoped to be in London on 28 March.

Vastly relieved, I went to the house in Grafton Way to tell Marlise, but was told she had left for North Africa and would not be back for two months.

On 28 March Mrs. Earnshaw telephoned and said she could not come to London today but I should not on any account hand the cat over until she had seen it. Even if it was not an Abyssinian, there was another aspect to this case. To abandon a cat was an offence at law. "I have passed many cases of abandonment to the RSPCA for prosecution." The stock defence in such cases was always that they thought the cat was being looked after by someone else, and it wasn't good enough. "Stand firm, and you will have all the animal welfare societies behind you. After all the veterinary care it has received while with you, it will certainly relapse if returned to unsuitable hands."

On 1 April, Cleo gave her first call, single and raucous. The Swiss boys were present, and gasped, "What is wrong?"

"Nothing is wrong. She is calling. It is to say, 'I am here.' "

"The female does that?"

"She will do it again and again." Long ago, I had for a short while had a Siamese, Bast. I had sometimes wondered if Tiutté was Bast come back to me. Bast had not been a happy cat and there was something similar in the personality. Cleo's call was of the Siamese type, though less strong. I had never heard Tiutté call. Perhaps British cats do not do it.

I took Cleo's calling as a sign of her recovery. When Tim telephoned me in the morning he said he could hear her calls over the telephone, and that when he played back the message I had left him yesterday on the answering machine the calls had recorded as a background to my voice. She was perfectly good tempered; just stood in the middle of the room, her head in the air, throat arched back, giving the calls. She had now to be guarded with particular care from White Tom.

Later that same morning, 2 April, Mrs. Earnshaw arrived. She was a small, slight person, shrunken with age but with inward authority. She looked at Cleo and said, "Very nice . . . very nice . . . very nice. If she had been bought with her pedigree, in good condition, she would have cost £20, minimum." It does not sound much today, but it was then.

"Do you believe they are descended from the sacred cats of ancient Egypt?"

"I do." After the siege of Khartoum, in 1885, she believed that not just one but several of these cats had been brought back by the men. There were too many testimonies to be disregarded, that these cats had been kept, within doors, very privately, as sacred. There were too many behavioural characteristics differentiating it from other cats for it to be just a breed, though breeders in England would have worked on it. "An African cat. Why shouldn't Africa have its cat?" She had spoken with Michaela Dennis who had told her that whilst she was on safari she had seen a small wild cat, no bigger than a domestic cat, run through the bush. Michaela had not known how significant that was, or she would have attempted to film it. In the 1920s there was an Exhibition of Middle Eastern Cats at a hall in Oxford Street, and Mrs. Earnshaw saw come in a party of men with dusky complexions. When they saw the Abyssinian in its show-pen, they started, bowed, and retreated from it backwards, their eyes downcast, so as not to commit the impertinence of looking at it. "Neither the cats nor the cat-worship have ever become extinct." I felt as though Mrs. Earnshaw was ancient Egyptian.

Looking at my other cats, she asked, "How does she get on with these?"

"It was traumatic at first, but they are getting used to each other."

She was surprised to see them living together peacefully. Abyssinians and others were difficult to mix. "Abyss are always top."

I was distressed to hear that. When I had brought Cleo in, it was as an extra. I did not want Tiutté, Bambina and Cynthia to be dominated by her. It was their home first.

I showed Mrs. Earnshaw my ancient Egyptian figurines, and opened for her my large-format facsimile reproduction of *The Papyrus of Ani*. As I turned the leaves I saw Cynthia lapping the milk from the silver jug, and apologised to Mrs. Earnshaw. "One is not supposed to notice that," she said softly. Then her eyes fell on Bambina. She looked at her quite intently, and said, "That's nice." The white, black, red and tan patches were beautifully distinct; she was artist-designed, and was most shapely, as was Cynthia too. "Oh my dear, you have been admired. And you don't know by whom you have been admired, admired, Bambi, by someone used to pedigree cats." Bambi came and stood on the book, and Mrs. Earnshaw moved her back gently, saying, "I don't think you're supposed to be on this book."

I found the depicted cat. Why had its tail been fluffed out into a golden ball? They had made a sun of it. Were the cats sacred to the sun?

Mrs. Earnshaw was looking at Cleo piercingly, and murmured, low, "I believe she is true bred."

But then she added a caution. In the progeny of an Abyssinian mated with any other cat, the characteristics of the Abyssinian predominated. Most Abyssinian kittens were males, which prevented apparent Abyssinians from becoming common, but even so perfect looking a cat as Cleo could have resulted from a mixed mating and in her descendents something else might show up. There were two Abyssinian stud cats, one in Dorset and one in Staffordshire, which would be nearer to where I was moving. She had told the story to Mrs. Bullock, who owned him. Mrs. Bullock would allow Cleo to visit her stud cat, but the kittens, being pedigrees on one side only would be non-pedigree, and so, even if they were mated to another stud cat, would their kittens. There would have to be three generations in which no other characteristic showed up, before Cleo could retrospectively be deemed Abyssinian and her descendents Abyssinian. What would I do with all the kittens of the intermediate generations? Nobody would buy them and to find homes for them would be a problem. "I should have her spayed."

It seemed sad, when she had all the points of the breed.

Mrs. Earnshaw's eyes narrowed as she looked at her, and she said, "Behind her origins there is a mystery. Or a secret."

I felt there was in her mind something she was reluctant to say, and wondered what it was.

The next day, 3 April, was Tim's and my usual "at home" day at Fuller dArch Smith, but Tim had to be away. The phone rang. I answered it. It was the woman. I said I had been advised not to continue conversations with her. Then, as this sounded rude, I gave her the telephone number of my solicitor. This was my tactical mistake. I hung up, and immediately the phone rang again and she asked me to repeat that number. I did. I hung up again and it rang again. "If it's about the cat, say I'm out," I said to one of our guests, and went out, to make it true. When I returned, the guest said it was about the cat but a man, this time. When told I was out, he said, "That's strange, I was talking to her just now." He added, "I'm just round the corner."

It was impossible he knew where we were and the recorded message on our answering machine did not include the firm's name.

Days passed without any further come-back, and at last there was a date for the exchange of contracts and my move to the country.

THE MOVE

THE MOVE was traumatic. Because of the quantity of the furniture they had to take, the clutter of books and paintings and the strange things such as the marble pillar, which Vilayat had given me because he could not take it back to France, the removers made two prior visits. The first was to pack the library. This did not disturb the cats too much as I kept them in the sitting-room. But, on the eve of the move they called to pack almost everything else. I said, "If you empty the study first, I can afterwards put the cats into that while you empty the front rooms." They could not do that. They said, "We have to pack in a certain order."

When the men went into the sitting-room I tried to get the cats into the study — which they had always been so eager to enter when not allowed — but first one, then another darted out. They cowered under the furniture and, as it was lifted off them, dashed from one disappearing refuge to another. They were so terrified I was afraid of their being permanently deranged. I kept telling the men not to let a cat run out past them through the door. I could see neither Tiutté nor Cleo and feared them lost. I stood clutching Bambina and Cynthia in my arms, both mad with terror, their hearts pounding and their claws sticking into me.

At last the men went. Tiutté and Cleo emerged from I know not where. There was left, now, nothing save the TV, the sofa and bed.

Tim was going up that evening, to stay near and get the keys from the vendors before they left in the morning. I had a last supper with the Swiss boys. Tano made an Italian dish with vegetables on a base of maize.

In the morning when I woke, I was able to place Tiutté in the basket and fasten the lid. At 8.00 on 18 April, 1975, Ivor Cook arrived, a friend who had volunteered to knock down my bookshelves and drive me up. The hammering was dreadful for the cats. Bambina I managed to put into one of the cardboard boxes, but Cynthia broke out of hers and I could do nothing but hold her in my arms, starting with terror at the sound of each blow. Cleo was so frantic I thought she was going out of her mind. She tried to go down the hole through which Tiutté had once bolted. I had blocked it up, but she managed to get between the inner part of the skirting and the wall. I called to Ivor to leave the shelves and come and get Cleo. "Under the sink, behind the skirting." He eased the skirting away from the wall and got hold of her, but then cried out. She had scratched him so deeply he had had to let go. He showed me the blood. Then the removal men arrived and they and Ivor together caught her on the window-sill, and, all grasping her, lowered her into the big linen-basket Tim had brought and fastened the strap.

I was still holding Cynthia, staring eyed. I returned her to the carton from which she had broken out, and, as it had been damaged, put string round it. All the cats were carried down to the car. There was a last minute call from my solicitor and, just as I was going down the stairs, a trunk-call from Paris, from Hélène Bouvard, to assure me that *"Tout s'arrangera"*. It was 11.00 when Ivor took the wheel and we pulled out of Whitfield Street.

We had still to call in at my solicitor's, for me to give him the keys, which he would give "Mine host" when he brought the cheque. I rejoined Ivor and the cats and we were on our way. On the M1, unexpectedly, we sighted our vans. One had the

280

furniture from the office. Now we no longer needed the map, but just followed in caravan, off the M1 on to the A6, and down the turn to Wymington. It was by my watch just 2.00 when we arrived. Tim was at the front door. He handed me the keys of my own house. The money had been wired from my solicitor to the vendor's at noon. "The carpets are down. There's a grey stranger. He's not sure if he approves of us." I thought he meant an old man. "Put the pillar on the patio," I told the men. After so many years of standing in my bedroom, pointlessly, it would have the setting for which it was destined.

I was carrying the cats in their containers upstairs. The new beds I had bought had already been installed, so there was no reason for the men to come into the spare bedroom in which I put them. I opened the lids of the containers, which revealed them shivering and cowering. Then I slipped out, but barricaded the door of that room.

Below, Ivor was already putting the shelves up again in my new study, hammering, hammering. I knew the cats were in terror.

The unloading was long. The books were unloaded on to the study floor. I was unpacking the box of brass animals my mother had brought from India; two were missing, the cow and the boar.

Tim said, "I peeped into the room. No cats! Then I saw they were all underneath the lid of the linen-basket, which was turned back to make a roof over them."

"All four of them under the lid?"

"All four."

The differences had been obliterated.

Ivor had at last finished hammering, so I opened the door of the cats' room, but they did not come down.

Tim made our dinner. I offered Ivor one of the guest-beds, but his wife was expecting him and he left when we finished eating, at 8.00.

Tim and I sat very quietly now. Suddenly Cleo appeared at the door of the sitting-room, and crouching low ran swiftly round it, then upstairs again.

Tim went upstairs and prevailed upon Bambina to move. Shortly afterwards she came down, followed by Cynthia. Together, they circled round the new sitting-room, sniffing at everything, recognising furniture they knew, excited but curious.

Cleo came down again. She was more nervous than Bambina or Cynthia, but this time she, too, stayed.

We put out food, and all three ate.

Only Tiutté did not come down. I carried food upstairs to her, but she did not eat it. She ran from what had been their room into what would be Tim's, and under the bed. When we went upstairs, Tim went to bed with her still underneath it, but left the door open in case she wished to go down. In the morning, when I opened the door of my room, she ran straight from under the bed in his room to under the bed in mine.

As I looked through the window into the garden below, I saw a smokey figure with green eyes. It was only then that I realised what Tim had meant by a "grey stranger". It was what fanciers call blue.

Whilst waiting for my arrival with the vans, Tim had spoken with the people next door. They had five cats but this was a strange one seeking a home.

"He's rather nice," I said. Yet it would be one more to feed.

We were both very careful to keep all doors to the outside closed, for my cats must not go out until they had been in this house long enough to think of it as their home, and return to it.

Tim left at mid-morning by the bus to Bedford, which stopped paces from my door. I returned and stood for the first time alone in my new home. Now I felt lonely.

It was the time to keep my promise to the little oak-tree. All through the winter I had been assuring it that I would plant it out into a garden. Now, with difficulty, I lifted the heavy pot and, taking care the cats did not get out, opened the door from the sitting-room onto the patio, and up the steps to the lawn, opposite the sitting-room window. I would not plant it out yet, in case the shock of transference from the centrally heated flat should kill it, but take it out at first during the hours of sunlight only.

My typing desk (which my mother had bought me) and those book-cases that were free-standing, were still on the patio with the pillar. Being careful not to let the cats out, I opened the study window and levered the book-cases up and over the sill, but I could not do this with the desk. It was wider than the window.

I telephoned Martin. He came, and said, "We shall have to re-route it, through the sitting-room and the passage." With three doors to negotiate, I made sure all the cats were upstairs, but he did glimpse Cynthia and said, "I haven't seen you before." We carried the desk together.

In the evening I wrote a letter to Jean-Louis and Tano, saying, "Only Tiutté has not eaten." Before I posted it I tried once more to tempt her, opened a fresh tin and placed the plate under my bed. Then I crouched down, and saw her beginning to eat. I was able to add a PS to the letter.

Before I went to bed I lifted it slightly, which caused her to come forth, and she went down to join the others.

The arrival of electricians on Monday to fix new points was a new alarm, and on Tuesday the telephone engineer sent them all flying. "Do you know what's under the bed?" I asked him. "Four cats." He never saw them. But in the afternoon, when all was quiet, they stole out again.

Cynthia was so sweetly confiding that, on an impulse, I carried her into the garden, holding her tight in my arms. It was the first time she had ever smelled fresh air. Only her ears and her nose were twitching. I sat down on the grass. She did not move from my lap when I ceased to hold her. I lay down on my back. She laid herself down on my stomach, stretching herself out along it, her forepaws between my breasts, only her head raised, her ears turning to catch every sound. There was a chirping of birds, and it was strange to her. Her nostrils quivered; the air was strong for her. She did not step off me. I was a boat, on the ocean of the grass. Its blades, faintly stirred by the breeze, were ocean waves. We were a thousand miles from shore, and I was the raft to which she clung.

We remained so for half an hour. I began to feel the damp beneath my back. To encourage her to make some move, I stroked her, tried to interest her in the grass. She put her two front feet down on to it, but quickly brought them up again. At my urging, she put her front feet down a second time, and then both hind feet. But then she stepped back quickly on to me.

"Sweet Cynthi, poor Cynthi! I am the only refuge you know, the only mother you know, the only security in a changing world."

The white-edged ears twitched, the little nose with the white blaze up the one side quivered; the grey-green eyes were large.

Very slowly and gently I changed my position, rolling over so that I lay on my side. As I rolled she changed the position of her paws, so that she was always on the part that was uppermost. At last she was standing on my hip. The boat having capsized, she was clinging to the keel. "Poor Cynthi!"

I sat up and clasped her in my arms. I stood up and walked with her slowly towards a flower-bed, holding her near to a tall wallflower. She was frightened of the wallflower, and retreated from it. "It's a flower, dearest. Smell it." She put her nose towards it but quickly retreated. I brought her back to the house. Bambi had been watching from the doorstep, but I had not carried her out and she had not quite the courage to step out unassisted. Each evening, when I sat on the sofa, Bambi sat on my feet, to prevent me from leaving: a guardian. Cynthia lay on my lap, Cleo on the arm of the sofa behind me and Tiutté under the sofa. I said to her, "You are a citizen of this house, Tiutté. You have your honoured place. You have not to hide." When I got up to go to bed, the kittens went back to the basket, and the last thing I saw before putting the light out was their two little faces pressed together, like the twin halves of one flower.

On Wednesday evening Tano rang. I told him of their fear of being taken out of doors and he suggested that instead of carrying them out I simply leave the door open.

On Thursday morning I did this, and stood outside to give them encouragement. Both of them approached it. They stood side by side, their feet exactly on the dividing line between the inside and the outside. Only their noses moved, as they smelled the air. How long they would have stayed so I do not know, but Grey Tom appeared and they both fled. I shut him out, but they rushed to the top of the house and under the bed. Bambina came down later, but Cynthia stayed there all the rest of the day.

In the evening, I was in my study, with Bambina in my arms, when we saw Grey Tom at the window. Bambina was so frightened she leapt from my arms and went to join Cynthia upstairs.

I tried calling Grey Tom Blue Tom but it did not work. Tim was right. He was Grey Tom, a grey ghost, grey menace, grey eminence jailing me. Now that he had found my female cats he never left my doors and windows. He was at the back-door, the sitting-room window, and, when I opened the front-door to someone who knocked, he was on the front step. When I went to my study to type, he was on the sill, directly in front of me, divided from me only by the glass, his green eyes goggling through it. Wherever he appeared, Bambina and Cynthia fled. But Tiutté and Cleo both leapt up to the inner side of the sill, wanting to join him. Bambina and Cynthia were virgins and fearful, Tiutté and Cleo had mated and were eager to mate again.

The following morning brought a letter from my solicitor. Usually I was glad to receive his letters, but as soon as I saw this one on the mat I knew it boded no good. Enclosed in it was a letter from the woman. I had to read it several times before I realised she was not actually asking for the cat back. She said it was Bramble Camilla and had a pedigree which she had mislaid but of which she would be able to obtain a duplicate. She was an animal nurse. The cat and its sister had been given to her, and when, last August, it had kittens, she gave one to a friend, Elizabeth, and left Bramble Camilla at "Elizabeth's house" until the kitten was old enough to be on its own. It was only when she called recently that she learned Elizabeth had disappeared. She would like to meet me, and mentioned her man friend.

The story was not the same as the man's. The man had said he had kept the kitten, and it was Bramble, together with her sister, whom he had given to Elizabeth. And then, a kitten is weaned in five or six weeks. If a kitten had been born in August and the cat lent only to suckle it, the cat could have been reclaimed in October at the latest. Yet when I took her to Lawson, on 24 January of this year, he had found milk in her teats, and Marlise had spoken of a litter of several kittens, who must have been born in December, after Elizabeth had left. Then, the phrase "Elizabeth's house" was misleading. That dreadful derelict house was not anybody's home. The people living in it had just crept in. If they had not found the lockless front-door they would probably have been sleeping rough. Elizabeth had been a squatter, like the rest of those there. Nobody could have thought it a proper place in which to leave a cat. Marlise had been right. Nobody had enquired about the cat in six months. If they had called, they would have found her, with her litter by White Tom.

I wondered into what sort of accommodation the woman and man had moved. If it was another "squat", I did not want them to have Cleo in it. I remembered Mrs. Earnshaw's warning that she could quickly relapse if returned to unsuitable hands; and I did not want the pair coming to my house at Wymington.

I wrote to my solicitor that if the woman could prove ownership he could offer her £20 for the cat with pedigree, or £5 without it. Before I posted it, I read it over the phone to Tim, and he thought it "very fair". I also posted a copy to Mrs. Earnshaw, who said £20 was "far too much. £10 at the outside." But by that time I had posted it.

One thing was good. Seeing Grey Tom had acted as a tonic to Tiutté. Having once sprung to the inner sill to try to join him she did not relapse but lost her desire to hide. She circulated again, shook off the beaten look and recovered her spirit. She was friends again with her kittens. Only, in feeding she would have eaten last, had I not given her a separate plate.

So I was grateful to Grey Tom. Since no pregnancy could result, I would have let Tiutté go out to him, but that I had looked at him in the sunlight and seen that his ears were cankered. Until I could get that treated, she would have to make do with flirting with him through the glass.

Then Cleo started calling. While still un-spayed, she must at all costs be kept from Grey Tom. In the evening of 26 April I had to go into the garden for something and as I re-entered, Cleo slipped out past me. Too late, I remembered Tim's warning, "Watch that door. Never open the garden door at night. If one goes out at night, you'll never get it."

I had never carried Cleo out and shown her the way back to the house. In the dark, how would she find it again? I would have to put up a LOST card in the village shop. I walked down the garden path, calling "Cleo! Cleo!" There was just the light of a full moon. On the end-wall, I glimpsed her; she could have jumped down to the farm. Then a cat appeared beneath me, its head in my hand. It was not Cleo. It was Grey Tom. At least, he was not mating her. Then I saw her again. She was coming to us. He went towards her, and now she stood between us, looking from one of us to the other, hesitating as to whom she should join. Then she was lost to both of us, in the shadows. I recognised in Grey Tom an ally. "Find her, Grey Tom. You can see in the dark, and perhaps smell her. Find her, for both of us."

He led me by the compost heap and the nettles. I could see nothing. Then there was something at my feet. It was Grey Tom. Cleo was beneath him. It was only because he had pinned her that I was able to take her by the scruff and carry her home. They had been together for only seconds. Had she been impregnated? Grey Tom followed us up the garden-path and sat outside the door, still eager. I saw that my shins were bleeding.

In the morning Grey Tom was maintaining his vigil. Because he had brought Cleo back to me I felt kindly towards him, and put out a plate of food and bowl of water. What should I do with him? On the step I examined him. Stella Reynolds, my next door neighbour, thought he was Russian Blue. I had thought British, but she was probably right, for his eyes were green and his coat peculiarly dense. Though the idea of breeding a cross might seduce, the kittens would be non-pedigree both sides, and there were tabby rings in his tail. A handsome cat, yet I had best have him neutered – and treated. His ears were sore, there was a sore on his back and a discharge from one of his eyes. But I could not find a vet in the directory.

On the 28th Cleo slipped out again and circled with Grey Tom in the garden. They were not mating but boxing. I tried to reach them but they went under the shed. I opened a tin of rabbit on a plate, set it in front of the shed and crouched above it. As his head appeared I grasped the scruff. He twisted every way and retreated back under the shed. I moved the plate further from it, so that he would have to come out further, and this time picked him up. He bit the back of my hand but I did not release him. I shut him into the passage between the front and the sitting-room door. Cleo had followed me in.

At 4.00 Martin and Helen called. I asked if they could take Grey Tom to their vet to be neutered.

"It needs an appointment," said Martin.

"Could you keep him till one can be made?"

"The dog would eat him." But he rang his own vet, a Mrs. Philp, in Sharnbrook, and made for me an appointment for 1 May.

Till then I would have to keep him in the shed. In its back-room I put a plate of food and bowl of water. Martin brought a linen-basket down and said, "You'd better put him into it as he knows you." Grey Tom, very forgiving, allowed me to put him in it. "You're a good cat," I said, as we closed the lid and carried him out, and into the inner room of the shed. I saw him beginning to eat before the door closed.

That evening as I opened the door to shake a mat out, Cleo rushed past me. A shadow, she crossed the grass. She ran to the shed, where Grey Tom was, and jumped up at the sides. When I tried to collect her she went under it. This time, I did not think I had lost her. Then, as I was going to bed, she was at the window, asking to be let in.

In the morning I looked at Grey Tom through the window of the shed. He miaowed to me. I opened another tin for him. He went straight to the food and allowed himself to be petted. I fed him each day, and gave him a name, Georgius. On 1 May I packed him into the basket and took him by taxi to Sharnbrook. Handing him to Mrs. Philp, I said, "Clean his ears and treat any other conditions you find. He's not my cat, he's a stray. It's chiefly for the protection of my cats."

When I called for him at 4.00 the basket was in the hall. I took him back by taxi and lest my cats should worry him, returned him for the night to the shed, which he knew, and opened a tin for him. He at once began to eat. Next morning I let him out of the shed and he came to the house. Cleo went to him. She had gone off call but they were still friends.

Bambina and Cynthia, however, though they began to assert themselves, were still frightened of him, and, relative to my cats, he was rather big for my house. When Martin called, he said, "Why don't you keep him as an outdoor cat? He has obviously been accustomed to live off the land. He will keep you free from mice. Because those little things couldn't catch mice. They're not big enough." (Martin would soon be in India and Africa writing and making screen plays about conservation of tigers and rhinoceroses.)

Later that afternoon I carried Cynthia out and sat down with her on the lawn. Georgius came up. In terror, she took her first plunge into grass and streaked across it to the house. On 4 May she crossed the garden for the first time, by the path. Then she went under the shed; but I went and stood at the far end of it and she took a flying leap over at least two feet of grass, into my arms. Bambina came out. It was her first sortie. On 5 May, Cynthia put her two front legs on to grass. I wrote to Tim, "It's the overcoming of the grass barrier."

Tiutté, all this time, had not left the house. It was on Tuesday, 6 May, late at night, that she rose and moved purposefully towards the garden door. I opened it and she went out. Through the window, I watched her walk up the path and sniff the night air, recovering her lost life. Would I ever see her again?

I went to my study to type, and suddenly she was on the sill. I opened the window, and so as not to deter her from entering, left the room. When I re-entered, she was inside, amongst my papers, but jumped out again. When I returned to the sitting-room she came on the sitting-room sill, but when I opened the door ran off. I had to shut her out, to go to bed.

In the morning I did not see her. Should I warn the boys she might turn up at Whitfield Street? I peered under the shed and could see her. It was raining, and as I walked back to the house she made a dash for it and was in before me. Tiutté knew her way *home*.

All the cats still fled from anyone strange, and on 13 May, when electricians called, Cynthia vanished. I asked people in the street, "Have you seen a tabby and white kitten?" So much of my love had gone into her that it came to me that, like the beauty of the cherry-tree, it was too piercing to last. When the electricians left, I found her within the house, but I now bought collars with name-discs for Bambina and Cynthia. Bambina hated hers so much I had not the heart to insist on her wearing it.

Cynthia now invited Cleo to play, putting her head down with forelegs outstretched. Cleo, however, did not play with any member of the Tiutté family. In the deck-chair, she and Georgius curled up together as a married couple.

On 15 May I received another letter from my solicitor. He had received a further phone call from the woman, asking for my telephone number, which he had refused to give her. She said she had not a pedigree but had a vaccination certificate, and estimated the value of the cat at £12. He had not told her of my offer of £20, but asked me now for a statement of what I had spent in vet's fees, food and care for the cat. I made out an account for £44, hoping this would put her off, for, he said, if she could prove ownership of the cat he did not see how I would be entitled to keep it. I did not think she could prove ownership but felt she might have accepted my offer of £20, which I would willingly have paid, even without pedigree. Cleo was on the garden's furthest wall and when I called to her she streaked towards me like a cheetah. She was, in Lawson's words, "my cat".

The following day, Martin called with his electric mower and cut my grass. The moment he had levelled it to a lawn, Cynthia walked across it. From then on, Bambina and she played on it, regardless.

On Saturday, 17 May the Swiss boys came to see me in my new home. As I brought them in through the door of the house, which I had called Steep House because it was on the steep part of the hill, they saw at once the kittens and Cleo. "Where is Tiutté?" asked Jean-Louis.

"Under the sofa."

"Of course," said Tano, affectionately mocking. He went down on his hands and knees and began wheedling.

"She cannot have forgotten Tano?" exclaimed Jean-Louis.

She had not forgotten Tano. Slowly, she came out to him.

I took them up to their rooms. Tano chose the one overlooking the church, Jean-Louis the one that looked over the garden. When I took them out into it, they asked, "Is it all yours?" as though some invisible line might divide it.

"It's all mine." I showed them the old and spreading lilac-tree, the venerable elder and the apple-trees in flower. My gardening would be all organic.

They had brought a bottle of red Chianti and Tano made us an Italian dish. They had not had to do with the Clarkes before I left, but I sent Mimi and Dave as well as them the little cat story up to the time of the move; that had brought them together, and they had been invited up to dinner, in memory of me, so to speak.

They took photographs of me and each other with all the cats in the garden. They would be leaving England at the end of June but gave me the addresses of their parents in Switzerland. "When we know where our bank will send us, you must come and stay with us." And so, with hugs and kisses, they were gone.

In the evening of that day Tiutté did a thing she had never done before. She stood before me and looked as though she were going to jump on my lap. She had never done more than sit beside me. "There's a first time for everything, Tiutté. There has always been a relationship between you and me. Come."

She placed her forepaws on my knees as if she were coming but did not have the courage to spring.

On the following evening, 19 May, she tried again, but did not manage it yet. "It's dreadful how the beginning conditions. You had a bad kittenhood and it is difficult for you to trust."

On 21 May I went to London for the first time since the move. Tim had booked us seats for *Love's Labour's Lost*. I had meant to shut all the cats in but could not see Tiutté when the taxi came to take me to Wellingborough railway station. On my return, when I opened the front door there were three faces to greet me, and I went into the garden to look for Tiutté. All I found were three half-grown rats laid out on the lawn. She did not come in till next morning.

In the garden I heard a squeal. Georgius was chasing Bambina. I flew at him. "That settles it. I will not have Bambina raped." I asked Ken and Stella if they would have him, and they did. I put wire up over the gate. I bought a cat-flap and on 23 May Martin came and fixed it. Bambina was the first to investigate it. Then Cynthia came up. I showed her it would open and put her through. Bambina saw, and went through unaided. She promptly came back and went out again; and in again and out. This experimentation confirmed my earlier impression of Bambina's special intelligence. Later in the evening Cleo went through. Tiutté did not, but after some days I noticed she, too, was using it.

My neighbour on the other side, Mrs. Short, asked me if I had seen a rat. She did not like to put poison down, but her Great Dane failed to get it. A few days later, in my garden I saw it. So did Tiutté. She ran after it and as it was about to disappear under the shed caught it and killed it with a single bite through the back of the neck.

The first to jump on to the wall at the end of the garden was Bambina. Perched on it she looked so beautiful I rejoiced. Cynthia tried to join her but could not quite manage it. Then she, too, did. I never thought it could bode danger for them.

SUMMER OF SUSPENSE

MAY 27 brought an envelope from my solicitor with a hand-written enclosure on purple note-paper. His covering letter set my mind at rest. "It will seem that the matter is now closed."

Cleo was mine and that was all that mattered. I wrote to the Swiss boys:

27 May, 1975
Dear Tano and Jean-Louis,
    I know that you will be as happy as I am to know that the affair vis-a-vis Miss — is now closed . . . she wrote a disagreeable little letter saying her patience was now exhausted and that she would not waste her time pursuing the matter further . . .

On 3 June I went to London again. I had to see my solicitor about something else, and he said, "I have received something further from Miss —."

"Oh no! I thought the matter was closed."

"So did I."

He handed me a paper. It was a summons to appear before the Bloomsbury and Marylebone Magistrates' Court charged with "wrongfully detaining a cat" and required to hand over either the cat or £500.

"Oh no!" At our denuded office I met Tim. Jean-Louis phoned me there, about a little cyprus tree which Tano and he had left Tim to plant out in my garden. . . . I had to interrupt him, to tell him what had happened.

He was stunned. "You have to give her up. It is too much for you."

The next morning Tano telephoned. He and Jean-Louis would give evidence for me. Their permits to stay in England expired at the end of the month and they had to be in Zürich on 1 July, but they would write statements for me. I doubted if the court would accept written statements. "Affidavits," he said. "Witnessed and sealed." He would telephone my lawyer.

I wrote to Mimi and Dave, at their new house near Diss.

I telephoned Mrs. Earnshaw. She was aghast. "She must be mad. The cat isn't worth anything at all. I've never known a case like this before." She would speak to the RSPCA Inspector and I should write to Mrs. Davies, the General Secretary of the Governing Council of the Cat Fancy. "They have a lawyer."

On Monday, Mimi phoned. "I just couldn't believe it when I got your letter. You took in a poor, starving little animal, and now you are being punished for it." She would come to court and give evidence that the cat was dying when I took it in.

"Bless you, Mimi."

It was Mrs. Davies I had first informed about Cleo. I wrote to her telling what had happened and she replied enclosing a letter from their solicitor, Mr. Parrot. He suggested mine should make a point of it that I had previously taken in three non-pedigree cats from compassion, and that I should pay £12 into court.

Mine sent me a copy of the Defence he had sent the court: Defendant disputed £500 as the value of the cat, purported Abyssinian, for which no pedigree had been produced; Defendant had three cats already; Defendant was unwilling to return cat to

conditions that might give rise to a prosecution for cruelty, but was willing to hand cat to the Cats' Protection League. The last I think he had added off his own bat.

He said the Swiss boys had telephoned him wanting to make affidavits, but he had told them he doubted whether in a case like this affidavits would be accepted. Unless they could come to court I had better forget their witness.

Tim came up on 12 June. We sat in the sun on the grass. He thought, as I did, Cleo was pregnant, and smiled to see the plump little body up-end to go through the flap. I told him what I was afraid of was the court fees, if the case went against me. They could not be estimated as they depended on the time taken.

In the meantime, I had been trying to find a place that would sell me two hens. On 15 June, Stella brought me two. They had been sold them as belonging to the same brood as others they had bought but the others pecked them and they would be happier with me: ruddy brown, Warren Studdlers. She brought them just after sundown, when they were ready to put head under wing. I called them Polly and Jennie. By the morning they had already laid, and Ken came over to make a pen for them using wire I had bought with pieces of wood and corrugated iron lying around. On the following morning, Cynthia was sitting before the pen, contemplating. During the day, all four cats went to the wire and contemplated. I would have liked to let the hens out but did not want them to kill the cats, or the cats them. "Neither usually occurs," said Ken.

After a few days I opened the door of the pen. Polly and Jenny stepped out, but then ran round the wire trying to find the way back in. Like the cats at first, they were afraid of the garden. They had, said Ken, before he bought them been kept with rows of others in a dark barn. Gradually they gained courage and walked across the lawn, always breast to breast, or in single file where bushes narrowed the way. The cats followed at a distance of three to four feet. At last, the two hens turned round to face the four cats, shoulder to shoulder.

On 20 June, Tano telephoned with tremendous news. Jean-Louis and he had been to the house in Grafton Way and had found Marlise. They had asked her back to their flat and told her about the trouble. She would write a statement saying the cat had been abandoned, give it to my lawyer, and, all-important, would go to court to give evidence from the box if a few of the boys would go with her. The man had called at the house a couple of months before and there had been fighting between him and one of the others there in which a knife had been drawn.

I wrote to my lawyer to tell him this marvellous news.

An appointment was made for me to meet Marlise at the boys' flat on 25 June at 4.30. I arrived the earlier, and Tano said, "That is a dreadful house. As the door opened one smelled the damp and the dirt."

Marlise came, fragile and humorous. She had in her hand a paper. It was signed by herself and seven of the other squatters:

> . . . Grafton Way,
> London W1

To whom it may concern: re Abyssinian cat "Bramble"

To the best of our knowledge the cat was looked after by Liz . . . who lived at . . . Grafton Way W1. She left, and the cat was then looked after by Stephen, who lived at . . . Grafton Way. Stephen was sent to prison and the cat was abandoned. The cat was starving and looking very ill.

A letter was sent to this address by Jean Overton Fuller offering to care for the cat, as she had seen it around our front-door. Nobody in the house wanted the cat and nobody else had made any attempt to feed it. The person claiming ownership of the animal had certainly not demonstrated any concern for it over a period of several months. All the people in the house agreed that it would be better for the cat to be kept by Jean Overton Fuller. Mrs. Fuller was interested in the cat's pedigree and was given the address of . . . [the man] who, to our knowledge, had given the cat to Liz . . . in Summer 1974.

> Nick . . .
> Laurel . . .
> Marlise . . .
> Tim . . .
> Sandy . . .
> Graham . . .
> Don . . .
> Collette . . .

I was immensely grateful and touched. That the squatters in that dreadful house, who could have shrugged off responsibility had done this, seemed to me wonderful.

Marlise said she had not wanted to go to court alone. Some weeks ago, the man had come to the house at about 2.00 in the morning, bringing about twenty people. The boys had tried to prevent his entering and one of them had threatened him with a knife. She did not wish to encounter him, but several of the boys who had signed the statement would be willing to surround her as she went to the court and even to go into the box as well.

None of them had heard of the woman claiming ownership of the cat. They supposed she must be a girl-friend of the man.

"I ought to have heeded your warning and not gone near him."

"He has several houses like this that he holds in a reign of terror."

"How?"

"He gets people into his power."

"How?"

"He picks up people who are lost, or in a bad way; and he helps them, but then they find they have to do things for him." Looking me very straight in the eyes, she said, "He is quite a dangerous man."

I felt she was being brave and when we parted I kissed her, and kissed the Swiss boys also for it would be the last time I saw them before they went back to Switzerland.

I felt very warmed and comforted, though like a character from some creepy fictional story about someone who through picking up a cat had stepped into the fringe of an underworld.

I wrote that night a long letter to my lawyer, and in the morning rang Tim. "People who are thought of as respectable can sometimes let one down, but these, of whom one would have expected nothing, have turned up trumps. Pure gold."

"Well there you are," he said.

A cat is adult at nine months, and as this was 26 June, as I made Bambina and Cynthia their breakfasts, I told them "Today you are no longer kittens, you are cats." They were still not big. I gave them delicacies and said, "There will be a further celebration when you are a year old."

The post brought a letter from my lawyer which sank my spirits. It had crossed with the one I wrote him last night and answered that I had written after Tano's phone call. I would have to consider the costs if after the preliminary hearing on 22 July (I had not realised it was only preliminary) the case went to court. If the woman could prove title he did not see how the court could award the cat to me except on compassionate grounds. Supposing what Marlise said was true. We could hardly guarantee a posse to protect her. How would I feel if she were stabbed with a knife because of witnessing for me. If he might express a view, this matter was getting out of proportion to what was at stake, a cat. He recommended I should give the cat to the Cats' Protection League or RSPCA, so that he could write to the woman that it was no longer in my possession.

I rang him but his secretary told me he had just gone on holiday. I had wanted to tell him Elizabeth must have thought the cat had been given, not lent, to her, since when she left for Cornwall she had given it to the boy Stephen. It was Stephen's arrest which had caused the abandonment. Didn't the police, when they arrested somebody, have a responsibility to enquire if he had any dependent animals for which provision should be made?

But what caused my heart to sink was that my witnesses, who were all prepared to go into the box for me on 22 July, might not be required for many months. They were ready *now*, but the passage of months could leave me without any of them.

Martin called in. I told him I was afraid of having to sell my house and be bankrupted to pay court fees; and that to take Cleo to Mrs. Earnshaw would mean a cross-country journey. Martin said there was an RSPCA branch near and gave me the number. After he had gone I dialled it and started to tell the story to the Inspector. I had got as far as it's having been brought me by Marlise when he interrupted, saying, "It's your cat."

"No. I haven't finished. . . ."

"No cruelty is involved. It's your cat."

"That is what is at issue . . . somebody else is claiming to be the owner."

"We are not concerned with disputes. Get a solicitor."

"I have one. He has advised me I should give the cat up to an animal welfare society."

"There is nothing we can do to help you."

He was so unsympathetic it came to me that he must have thought I was a heartless owner trying to get rid of a cat. Later somebody told me the RSPCA put down most of the cats it took in. If I had known that, I would never have offered it Cleo.

I wrote to Mrs. Earnshaw and, on the following day, unable to bear the suspense, phoned her. "Have you received a letter from me today?"

"Yes."

"Can you take Cleo?"

"Yes." I could have embraced her. She was sorry I was not fighting the case. She would have given evidence for me. "I don't see how you could lose."

My lawyer considered the risk too great, he wanted me to hand the cat to an animal welfare society and that would be the end of it.

"It will not be the end of it," she said. "They could come against us. We couldn't say we owned the cat." The purpose of the CPL was to find suitable homes for cats. Her idea of a suitable home was with me. If she offered Cleo to other people she could not disguise from them that she was the object of a law-suit.

"But will you take her?" I pressed, anxious again.

"Yes." She had at the moment no vacancy in her pens, but hoped to home some of the occupants soon, and it would be better to let her kittens be born, and then to move all together. She had friends in Northampton who could drive them down.

"Bless you!"

There was only one pang. Cleo was beginning to attach to me and I was having to withdraw from a link that would have deepened.

We talked of cats' matings and I wondered if having them selected instead of being allowed to choose their own affected their characters. "I will tell you a story," she said. She had a maiden Abyssinian queen. She sent her several times to stud but the maiden refused to let the stud approach her. "With cats, the female has to be willing. If she insists on facing the male and uses her forepaw to strike at him, he risks his eyes if he persists. I decided to let her choose her own mate, for the first time. I released her into the garden." She became pregnant. "I had no doubt that the father was a ginger tom who used to cross the garden." All the kittens were, to look at, nice Abyssinians, but one, whom she called Peter, was of outstanding beauty. "Just a beautiful *warm* tone" to the ground colouring. As he was non-pedigree on his father's side, he could neither be exhibited nor his services used to sire kittens by pedigree Abyssinian queens. There was nothing she could do with him but keep him as a pet. He had the most endearing disposition, affectionate and intelligent. Subsequently, that queen who had borne him was successfully mated to pedigree Abyssinian studs and bore kittens that were exhibited and won prizes. "But none of them a patch on Peter, none of them to compare with Peter, none of them with his character and special beauty — the best cat I ever bred."

On 2 July in the evening Cleo became suddenly restless, walking up and down, looking me straight in the eyes and miaowing loudly as if in pain and wanting me to do something about it. That she was trusting me made it more terrible that I was planning to part with her. She made rushes at the other cats, growling to drive them away, then turned round upon herself, trying to pull her kittens out. I hoped they were not too big. At 10.20 the first was born: light fawn feet, with a little fawn on the underparts and on the bridge of the nose, the rest blue; one could say, fawn below, blue above. Stella had asked me to let her know when the kittens were coming and I fetched her. It was 11.03 when the second came, of the same pattern but deeper blue. We thought that was all there were going to be, and I went to the study to write to Jean-Louis and Tano that Cleo had borne two kittens. As I came back to the sitting-room I saw that there was a third like the first, so I was able to add a PS before posting it. It was after midnight that I saw there was a fourth, much smaller than the others but more like Cleo. But Cleo was not washing it. She appeared too exhausted to care for it and I doubted if it would live.

In the morning, when I came down, Cleo was standing before the door to the inner passage, waiting for me, instead of in the basket with her kittens. They were less active than the night before and I feared she was not feeding them. She ran inconsequently about the house and garden and the last little one still had not been washed. I placed them against her teats but she would not stay with them, and I had to catch a train from Wellingborough to see Tim.

"What are they like?" he asked.

"Blue with fawn boots."

"All of them?"

"All but one."

"They must look rather odd."

"They do." I doubted if they would be alive when I got back.

Yet they were, and they were looking better. Cleo was sitting with them and had cleaned the youngest.

Mrs. Earnshaw was shocked by my description of Cleo's kittens. "I don't think she can be true bred. They should all have looked like her." Blue was recessive, whereas

Abyssinian was dominant even over tabby, the dominant colouration in British cats. "Abyss dominates all." What kept their numbers small was that their kittens were nearly all males. Marlise had told me some of Cleo's previous kittens were white, like White Tom. That should not have been, either. If Cleo's kittens took after their fathers, there was, despite her appearance, very little Abyssinian blood in her, Mrs. Earnshaw said.

What had she meant when she said at Whitfield Street that behind *her* was "a mystery — or a secret"?

She was slow in answering, spacing her words with caution. "Most cat-breeders are cat-lovers. That's what makes them think of taking it up. But then ambition and money come into it, and there are bad hats. . . ."

"What do bad hats do?"

There was a silence. Then she said, "I have always tried to breed the most beautiful animal of its kind, matching the best Abyssinians so as to balance and correct any small fault either might have. I have never sought to originate something new."

"Like a red bluebell or blue daffodil?"

"Yes. I prefer things with the natural characteristics of their kind." Experimental breeding must produce kittens few if any of which would combine just those characteristics of the parents of which the combination was sought. What was done with the others? It would be too horrible to think that anyone deliberately bred kittens to be put down. Vets would not like to keep putting down litters brought by the same person and would ask questions, and the Cats Protection League would not take kindly to having deliberately bred kittens dumped on them. The usual answer was, "Homes were found for them." Homes with people too ignorant to ask questions. With regard to Cleo, there were two possibilities. She could be the result of an accidental mis-mating, but then Mrs. Earnshaw would have thought that a genuine Abyssinian breeder would have dropped a line to her, saying, "One of my queens has mis-mated." That left the other, less pleasant possibility she had had in mind from the beginning. "Somebody is *doing* things with Abyssinians."

When I told Stella, she said, "Well, at least we now know why there isn't a pedigree. I wonder if that changes anything?"

The kittens could, perhaps, be exhibits in court, with Mrs. Earnshaw as expert witness to say the cat who bore those could never have had a pedigree. Stella was witness they were Cleo's.

Meanwhile, there was country life. Before I had known I would be given two hens, I had asked Martin if he could find a supplier of six, and on 4 July a crate arrived, full of clucking noises. Six white hens were in it, which flapped out, frightened. Two ran straight out over the crumbling garden wall at the back. Stella helped me search for them in the outbuildings of the farm below and retrieved one, wrapping it in a towel to prevent its kicking as we brought it back. In the morning, when I got up I saw the pen contained all six. Stella had found the other and dropped it over the wall. She brought a long rectangular box. "Big enough for them all to lay their eggs in."

When I went over later, Georgius was in it. I removed him, but found him there each day. The hens laid in the crevice between the box and the wall.

The white hens had speckles enabling me to distinguish them. I named them, in order of whiteness, Albi, Blanche, Speck, Maisie, Dulcie and Susan — Susan had quite a bit of mottling. Ken warned me, "They'll scratch up everything you've planted. Hens and gardens don't mix." Yet, though there was the pen, I liked having them about me. Polly and Jenny were the first to set feet over the step into the sitting-room. They pecked up not only the crumbs but the sawdust left by the electricians, from deep in the pile. But then the white ones came in, too, and it was rather much.

Working close to the earth was wholesome yet the law-suit nagged. On 8 July, by the broad-beans, I sat on my heels and said to myself I should ask the Masters of Wisdom what I had done wrong – for I must have done something wrong to be having all this trouble – and what I should do to put it right. The answer came more quickly than I had expected – I had refused human contact: the woman did not want the cat: she was insulted by my refusing to meet her and wanted to draw me out of my fastness. I wrote to my lawyer asking him to offer her an interview with me, in his office.

Cleo was still nursing her kittens. Tiutté had resumed her growling slightly yet did not attack them. She cried quietly to herself. It was hard for her; she could, again, have been the perfect mother.

A few days later, going to fetch something from my bedroom in the afternoon, I found Cynthia had got shut into it. She was standing on the corner of the dressing-table nearest to the door, shrieking for deliverance, and continued her crying even after I had gathered her into my arms. I crooned words to her that began to form themselves into a poem:

> "If I am still in some way connected
> With an inconceivably remote being
> On a distant star,
> Who taught me when I had four paws,
> May you, when in an inconceivably remote future,
> You have a mind like mine,
> And problems like mine,
> Know that there is one who however far distant,
> Hears your call."

I lowered my head to touch with it the little furry tabby-and-white head, murmuring, "Now we are on the same globe, at the same place, at the same time. We must make the most of it." Why did I speak as though our time was measured?

Cleo's kittens were three boys, who had opened their eyes, and – the last born – a little girl, whose eyes did not open till 15 July, and then only partly. She was much the prettiest, yet I feared she would be delicate.

On 16 July, on the way from my bath to my bed, I took the usual last look round the cat world. Bambina was in the round basket. Tiutté and Cynthia were on the couch. But neither Cleo nor her kittens were in their basket. I looked all over the house for them. Hot from my bath I dared not search the garden, and had to go to my bed.

In the morning, Cleo was there but no kittens. They were not big enough yet to have walked. I searched the garden, the hen-run, the shed, and peered under the shed with a torch. Cleo accompanied me, then went to sleep on the lawn. I feared the kittens would die from her not feeding them. "What have you done with them?"

At lunch-time I went indoors. A white hen was in the basket where the kittens had been. There was an egg beneath.

Cleo reappeared. She went to the basket where the kittens had been, as though looking for them. Now she wandered about as though bereft, came up to me and miaowed. She wanted me to find them. As I could not, and she had had no breakfast, I opened her a tin of cat-food but she would not eat; went back to the basket where the kittens had been.

At 6.00 p.m. I went up to my bedroom for something and found Cleo in it. She was standing looking at the wardrobe, and on a sudden thought I opened it. The kittens were all inside, on the floor, on my dresses, alive and moving. I had slept with them, unknowing, having closed the wardrobe door. They had been there at least eighteen hours.

I gathered them up in a big handful and carried them downstairs and put them in their basket. Cleo was still discontented and trying to carry them upstairs again, but at last she settled down with them and gave them suck.

They began rearing up against the side of the basket, and it would not be long before they were over the rim. To see them better I carried them out into the sun with a magnifying glass. Using this, I could see that the hairs on the boys were separately banded, after the Abyssinian fashion: light blue at the base, then band of darker blue, then cream. "Blue Abyssinians!" I said ruefully. If it had not been for the boots, they would not have been too bad; the little girl was better, a greyer version of her mother — but with Georgius's rings round her tail.

On 19 July Mrs. Earnshaw rang. "I don't want to drag Cleo and her kittens down here for nothing, but I could take them now."

I would have fallen on her neck with relief, but, I told her, I had just received word from my lawyer, back from his holiday, sounding more cheerful. I should make no drastic move until 22 July, when he would attend the preliminary hearing. If the woman did not show up, no court fees would be incurred and the case would be struck off.

Mrs. Earnshaw was relieved. The 22nd was only three days away, and if need be she could still take the family after that.

On the following morning I had given the cats their breakfast when I noticed Albi looking into the basket where the kittens were. Anxious for their eyes in case she pecked, I gathered them up. "It will only take a minute for her to lay and then you can go back."

The Reynolds returned from a short while away and Stella ran towards the basket and picked up the little girl, exclaiming, "Ah, pretty, pretty!"

"Would you like to have that one?"

"Yes."

Later she told me Charles (their son) would like to have "one of the little grey ones". He asked me to choose, and I chose him the second born, which seemed the most affectionate. Charles took over my name of Blueboy for him; Stella first called hers Sheba, but they settled down to Little Girl and Little Boy.

22 July was tense. Trying to take my mind off it, I made my first oil-painting of Cynthia, standing on a stone slab in the lawn on which a swing had stood. At 5.00, unable to bear it longer, I telephoned my lawyer's office to find if he had returned from court. He answered, "The hearing was adjourned."

The woman had been there, and the man, both "very personable". He had spoken with them and told them I offered an interview. Friday 25 July at 2.00 had been agreed. This would be completely open-ended but she would like me to bring the cat "for identification". If she said when she saw it, it was not her cat, that would be the end of it; it would let her withdraw without losing face.

On the morning of the 25th I was getting ready to leave the house with Cleo when the telephone rang. It was my lawyer's secretary, to say the woman had rung to say she had chicken-pox.

When I went next door to tell the Reynolds, Ken said, "She's chickened out."

Dare I believe this? It came to me quietly that I should not hear from the woman again. It was over.

A CULMINATION

IT HAPPENED THAT on the evening of the following day, 23 July, Cynthia came and sat beside me on the red sofa at a moment when there was near my hand a red crayon and a canvassed board for painting in oils. I used the red crayon to draw her outline – half-recumbent with head raised – on the board. That red crayon would merge with crimson oil-paint for the sofa, and I could fill in her face and markings from the many sketches I had made in the note-books. The paints were outside in the shed, which in the beginning I used as a studio, and when I went out to it the next morning Cynthia followed me and walked about amongst my paints, giving me the opportunity to refresh my memory of how she was built. She jumped on to my shoulder whilst I was working on her face. "My dear, it isn't the usual place for the model. I have known humans who kept jumping up to see how the portrait was going, but to have one's sitter on one's shoulder looking at it with me while I work. . . ." Though done at great speed, it was the first of the paintings of the cats that I was pleased with.

It was late in the evening of 26 July when suddenly I could see neither Bambina nor Cynthia. I went out with a torch but could not find them in the garden. I had put wire below and above the gate to the Lane, and had never known them go in that direction of the Rushden Road. Then I found them in the front bedroom, curled up together. Bambina went downstairs to join her mother, but Cynthia followed me into my room. I did not normally allow them into my room while I slept, but having had a fright, when I missed them both, I had not the heart to eject her, "But what will happen in the morning, when I do my pranayama?"

The Sunday bells were pealing when I woke with her at my feet. In my nightgown, I seated myself on the floor cross-legged. She sat on my crossed legs. "Dear, do you think you can sit very still? I'll ask a blessing for you. Master bless a little person, the little person on my knee, Cynthia."

She remained absolutely still, and we went down together.

Albi came in early, and to save Cleo's kittens I scooped them out of the basket on to the sofa. Polly and Jenny came in, and found my half-pound of butter. Then the rest of the white hens came in. I was alarmed for the kittens. Talk about "a bull in a china shop", eight hens taking to flight in my sitting-room as I flapped them out were rather much. Then I saw that Cynthia did not like finding Cleo's kittens on the sofa, which she regarded as usurpation of her privilege. She began to growl. A lot of the smoke was curling about the flame. I returned the kittens to their basket.

On 30 July, Jason, the first born of Cleo's kittens, climbed out of the basket. He was so pleased with his accomplishment that he crawled back and out again five times. Then the others followed. Cleo was out, and I saw the Little Girl making towards Tiutté. I was appalled." That's not your mother!" Tiutté slashed at her, but the little thing picked herself up and staggered towards her again. Tiutté fled. That night I saw they were all four making towards Cynthia. She growled, felt herself encircled, and fled, through the cat-flap and out into the night. I went out into the darkness calling, "Cynthi, Cynthia. . . ." Cleo followed at my heel, thinking I was calling her. Cynthia appeared, white on the path between the vegetables. I gathered her up and took her to my bedroom with me. "This is not meant to be a regular practice." I slept but she kept waking me by purring.

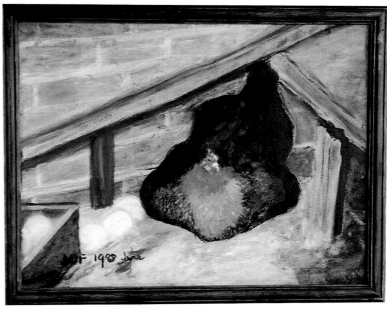

That evening, I had put a saucer of milk for Tiutté, and she was lapping it when she became aware that Cleo had come up and was seated facing her. Tiutté stopped for a moment, hesitating as to whether she should give way, but after a moment resumed and finished lapping. I poured a little more. Tiutté and Cleo now faced each other across the milk, each unable to move forward because the other was there. For a long time they remained motionless, the stasis too tense to be broken. Then Tiutté began to move forward, very slowly. Would she be the one to drink first? I had been sad at seeing her for so long the under-cat, and I hoped she would. Unbelievably, she brought her nose to the saucer, lapped till all was gone and then turned away. Cleo came up and licked the dampness that was left.

That evening, Cynthia wanted to follow me again to my room, but I said, "I don't want to separate you from Bambina. You, whose faces are the two halves of one flower, could be companions for ever." But after I had gone to bed there was such a pushing at my door that I had to let her in. In the morning, when I took off my nightdress she tried to take one of my nipples in her teeth. I was afraid of being injured, and said, "I have no milk to give you but I love you."

Below, at breakfast, I was startled by Tiutté and Cleo's fighting. It was the first time they had struck one another. Before I could part them, they disappeared through the garden door. Both returned uninjured.

That night when I went upstairs I found both the sisters, Bambina on my bed and Cynthia on the ironing-table by the open window. "Perhaps on this very hot night we shall both sleep more coolly in rooms near to each other." Day after day the temperature had risen to over 90. Tiutté had joined us and in the morning Cleo came up too.

That was the beginning of the "morning meditation class". In the morning, as I seated myself in the lotus position, all four cats settled round me, as though they accepted that this was some special reunion. I say "settled", but Bambina tended to frolic. "When *you* can still your vibrations," I said to her, "That will be the day!"

Yet nice as it was to have them assembled round me in the morning, I did find that they woke me from my sleep so often that it was taking too much out of me.

Returning in the afternoon from the Lane to the house, I saw Bambina sitting on the gate. I had not meant the cats to be able to climb that, but her beauty took my breath. Her two white forelegs like slender pillars, she held herself so high, I wanted to paint that, yet doubted that I could capture in paint that delicacy, that superb refinement and grace.

But now I was trying to find homes for Cleo's kittens, Jason and Tertius. A card in a shop window, "Abyssinian/Blue cross, free to good homes" brought several applications but from unsuitable people. One wanted a fluffy Persian type, others had small children. Mrs. Earnshaw had warned me against letting them go to homes where there were small children. "They pull their tails and tweak their whiskers." Unfortunately, it was for their children some people seemed to want them. I wanted adults, who would appreciate them as companions.

Tim was coming up on 21 August. Just as I was leaving to meet him, a woman came and chose Tertius. . . . I climbed the hill and met Tim as he came off the bus at Wymington Turn. The weather was so glorious that we made a salad lunch on the lawn. "Cheese — if you can bear to eat cheese in the presence of Cleo?" He passed some to her, but she snatched the rest of it from his hand. "She is a thief," I said. "The strangest things have appeared on my vegetarian lawn. One morning, it was the remains of a lamb-chop. Since then, an ox-tail."

"Somebody must leave their kitchen window open!"

Just then one of the white hens snatched from his hand the bread from which Cleo had already removed the cheese. So we went indoors, and heard the bell when the woman brought Tertius back. I put a saucer of milk down for him and he ran to it so fast that Tim said, "They can't have given him anything to eat all day." So, he saw Cleo reunited with all her kittens. As they swarmed all over her, one closing her eye with his foot, Tim said, "This is supposed to be your fulfilment though you don't look as though you were enjoying it."

I thought the kittening had been too soon after the previous one, and had taken too much of her strength.

The Reynolds now took Little Girl and Little Boy. Georgius, Stella told me, was very pleased to see Cleo when she went to visit them. They rubbed noses.

Cleo could now become pregnant again and I wrote to my lawyer asking if I could lay myself open to any further legal procedings by having her spayed. He wrote back saying he thought I should do, the case would eventually be struck off, he regarded it as closed and tendered his bill, for £30, which was not too bad.

In the newspapers I read that there was an outbreak of feline infectious enteritis, so packed all my cats into baskets and took them by taxi to Mrs. Philp. When I opened the one in which I had put Bambina and Cynthia, there was only Bambina. "There's one missing!" I cried. She was sure I would find her on my return. It was too early to give booster vaccinations to Tiutté and her kittens, but she inoculated Cleo and gave me a date on which to bring her back to be spayed. When the taxi brought me back, Cynthia was sitting on the lawn.

The annual exhibition of the Chelsea Art Society was usually in September, and when Tim had come I had asked him, "If I send in this year, which of my pictures do you think is the best?" "Cynthia," he had replied, meaning on the red sofa. I thought it successful, but would the judges? The competition is fierce. Sending In Day was 1 September, and I took down three, Cynthia, marked in the price column NFS (Not for Sale), a flower-piece and a landscape, and handed them in at the Chenil Galleries. The notification was supposed to arrive on Thursday 4 September, but I had to leave in the morning before the post arrived, as it was Tim's and my At Home day in the office we were still trying to get rid of. From the office I phoned the Secretary. "I live in the country and the card had not arrived when I left this morning to come to London. I can call now if there are rejects to collect or a hanging fee to be paid. Can you check for me?"

"One has been accepted," he said.

"Which one?"

"*Cynthia*."

I took a taxi to the gallery, to collect the other two. One was not supposed to see in, but I managed to get a pre-Private View peep and saw that *Cynthia* was nicely hung.

I came back by the next coach, and its original was in the garden to meet me. "Oh Cynthia, if you could only know that your portrait now hangs in the Chelsea Arts!"

That night her behaviour was extraordinary. She came on to my bed and purred, and purred and purred, not just for a few minutes but hour after hour, walking up and down my chest, licking my face and ears and purring into them so loudly that it seemed like a great noise. The purring became so strong that I was afraid the little heart would burst from the throbbing. "Darling, what is it? What is it?" I remembered having given her the Master's blessing and hoped it had not been too much for her. She was in an ecstasy of joy that knew no abatement. I carried her into one of the other bedrooms, but she hurled herself again and again against the door, until I let her back into mine, when again she started the licking of my face and purring. At 7.00 in the morning, feeling I must try to get some sleep, I carried her down into the sitting-room, but during that last hour I did not sleep, and when I came down at 8.00, she flung herself into my arms. Over breakfast she quietened, and later in the morning slept.

Cleo's appointment was for 11 September, and just before I set out for it, a Mrs. Philpot and a Mrs. Green called. They were next-door neighbours in Rushden and one of them grieving for a Siamese who had died aged sixteen years. They had thought that rather than attempt to replace, they would have something a little different. The two kittens remaining with Cleo would be able to visit each other in their new homes across the wall dividing their gardens. So, I gave them into the right kind of hands, and took Cleo to her appointment. At 4.00, when I called, the hot weather had broken, it was wet and cold and as I carried the basket out I feared her getting a chill after her operation. But when we were home, she stepped out of it looking well; she was affectionate and next morning began to purr.

Now that Cleo's kittens were gone, Tiutté ceased to resent her. To four peaceful cats, I said, "So now there are just five of us again, as we used to be."

The little oak-tree had loved the fresh air and I had ceased bringing it in at nights. When its leaves fell, I would plant it out. Because of the hot summer I feared the earth would be hard, and began digging the hole. Also I thought about that stone slab in the lawn, and while I dug the oak-tree's hole flexed my muscles for getting up the slab. I had to cut away the grass that had grown over it and then dig down till the fork went under it. At first it seemed immobile, but in the end I got it up. It was in the shape of a tomb. What should I do with it – or with the space beneath? Perhaps I could hollow it out to make a pool for goldfish. The slab lay on the grass, next to the space from which I had dug it.

The exhibition closed on 20 September, when I went down to collect *Cynthia*. One of my astrologer friends was there and asked if I had noticed the current Saturn-Uranus square affected my Sun, and what I thought to do about it. "Try to live rightly, avoid precipitating karma." I had prayed for all those dear to me.

She said, "If anything's going to happen you will know by the end of October."

When I got back, all the cats were waiting for me. I showed Cynthia her portrait again and returned it to its place on the wall.

That evening, as I sat on the sofa, Tiutté stepped up and sat down on my knee. "There's a first time for everything, Tiutté. After all these years!"

The next day, 21 September, I found Cynthia curled up in a large-brimmed picture-hat I had bought. She looked so pretty in it that I had not the heart to turn her out. "Nothing is too good for you. It was made for you, darling."

26 September would be the first birthday of Bambina and Cynthia. I would give them special delicacies and tell them, "You are one, today."

In the evening of the 21st, Cynthia was on the sofa beside me. I was aware of her two white paws on the green sleeve of a woolly I was wearing, white paws on my arm. It was the last I ever saw of her.

I thought she had only gone into the garden to relieve herself but in the morning, of the 22nd, only the other three were there. I opened a tin for them and then went out, calling, "Cynthi, Cynthi, Cynthi! Come in and have your breakfast before the others eat it all."

I said to myself, "I have been through all this before . . . when she disappeared after the electricians came, when she ran away from Cleo's kittens, when I took her to the vet and she was not in the basket . . . each time she reappeared."

I went in and made coffee. Yet though I tried to reassure myself I remembered that feeling I had had of foreboding when she vanished after the electricians came, "The beauty of it is too great, she will be taken from me."

I looked in every room of the house and again in the garden. I changed into trousers and went through the nettles, under the elder-bushes and brambles. I went down to the farm and obtained permission to search the shed in which they kept their machinery. "Cynthi! Cynthi!"

She was not in the Reynolds' garden, nor in the Shorts'. At last I thought of that other house, between the Shorts' and the farm, its front garden going down to the Rushden Road. I knocked and said, "I've lost my cat." The owner let me look in her back-garden, and there I found her, lying flat. Hoping she might be only sleeping, I rushed towards her. She was dead.

I carried her back in my arms. I thought she might have taken poison, and tried to pour water into her mouth to wash it out, in case she was still alive. "I love you. If you are still in your body, know I love you." But her left eye was turned in a peculiar way, her teeth were set, and her tongue protruded slightly from one side. I had been trying to work her limbs, resisting the *rigor mortis*, but now I called a taxi. Ken saw us while I was waiting for it, and said, "She's dead." But I gave the driver the address of Mrs. Philp's new surgery, in Rushden. All the way, I prayed for her.

Mrs. Philp saw me at once, but said, "She's dead. She has been hit by a car. It was instantaneous."

But, from the road, where she must have been hit, she had run up through the garden of that house, trying to get back to my house, her home. . . .

Mrs. Philp offered to dispose of the body, and when I said I would rather take her home, gave me a box in which to carry her.

Carrying her in the open box, I walked back, all the way from Rushden. In case the spirit was not yet quite gone, she should have her time to lie in state, and I carried her into my study. There, I telephoned Tim. He was out, but I told him on our answering machine. Then I wrote to the Swiss boys. They would be terribly upset. I wrote to Mrs. Earnshaw. I wrote to Mimi . . . I felt I had to inform everyone who had known her.

The little body was still with me. It was quite cold, now. Where should I place it? Then I noticed that stone slab, lying beside the space I had created when I got it up. I knew, now, what I had to do with that space. I had to dig a hole in it within which to place the coffin, and then get the slab — the slab on which she had stood when I made that first painting of her — back over it, to be the stone of her tomb.

While I was doing this, Bambina came up.

A MONTH AND A DAY

IN MY SADNESS, it was Tiutté who gave me the most comfort. In those first hours, she sat beside me, silent, yet showing her affection more than usual, as though she knew there was sorrow for us to share.

When Tano telephoned, he said, "That it should be *that* one!" As he talked, it came to me that he was saying things that related only to Pearl. He was thinking of Cynthia as Pearl. Perhaps it was just a slip of the memory, or perhaps an intuition of the truth. I wished, now, that I had not had Tiutté spayed, and so prevented her from bearing more kittens, into one of which she could reincarnate again.

It was on the afternoon of the following day that I felt quite suddenly that she was not in the grave but in my arms. Why should a little dependent soul go off and lose itself in space for aeons (as Leadbeater's books seemed to teach)? I carried her about with me.

A slight breeze put lines into my head:

> Violets at her head
> And snowdrops at her feet
> The last cadaver lies;
> But she is warm against my breast,
> The resurrected paws,
> Blest eyes.

I would call it, "For my Little Cat, Cynthia, 16.9.1974-22.9.1975"; I would set the flowers in the spring.

It seemed to me that it must have been after daylight that she had been hit, since she was still warm when I found her, which must have been about 10.00 or 10.30. I remembered how proud I had been when I saw first Bambina, then Cynthia, jump up on to that wall at the back — the wall that led to the fatal garden. For Bambina's protection, I ordered an enormous coil of wire to go right along it, but it took time to arrive, during which I could only put up make-shift barriers.

On 23 October when I came downstairs I could not see Bambina. "Oh no! It's not going to be like the Ten Little Nigger Boys!" I ran out into the garden, calling "Bambi! Bambi! Bambi!" It was like a repetition of that dreadful morning. . . .

Back in the sitting-room I found her. She must have been there all the time, only, she was crouched on the floor, half-hidden by the sofa, with blood on her face.

I bathed it with water and calendula lotion. Except that she quivered a little, she was almost without motion. At first I thought another cat had scratched her, but I did not like the way her tongue was hanging out. Then I saw there was oil on her fur.

I called a taxi and rushed her to Mrs. Philp. She said, "Those are road burns. She has been hit by a car." Hit from behind, pitching her forward on to one side of her face, taking the skin off her left cheek-bone and lip. Mrs. Philp gave her penicillin, and said, "She has a good colour inside her mouth. She will make a complete recovery."

After this, I would lock her in at nights, even after the wire came. I brought her back in the taxi. Yet, at home, she simply sat. It was as though she was still quite dazed and I could not persuade her to take any nourishment.

It was the same on the following day; she would take neither food, milk, Complan

47

nor water. It was as though she were in a coma. I went into the garden and did some hours digging (having shut her in) and when I returned I sat on the floor to change my shoes, and, being very tired, lay on my back on the floor. I did not actually fall asleep, yet it was almost like being wakened from sleep when I became conscious of a little cat sitting on my chest, purring. "Only Cynthia does that." I was being kneeded with paws and the purring was loud. I opened my eyes. It was Bambina. I was amazed, for she had not eaten or given any movement in all these hours. When I changed my position, rolling over on my hip, she moved her paws so as to keep on top of the rolling ship, as Cynthia had, that first day on the grass.

Ever so gently I said to her, "If you are strong enough to knead me and purr, perhaps you are well enough to lap a little milk." I poured her out a saucer and she lapped it. She was a changed cat. I closed the cat-flap well before dusk. "You have to be kept safe, inside."

It was late in the evening, on the upstairs landing, at 11.45 that, when I bent for something, she jumped on my back, "Only Cynthia jumps on my back. . . ."

I asked for a sign. Yet what could be a sign more certain than that I had had? If she jumped on to the top of the wardrobe which only Cynthia did. . . . She jumped on to the top of the wardrobe.

But then she came down, and pushed her head up under my left arm-pit. That was a thing which Cynthia never did. Only Bambina did that.

BAMBINA, MY DAUGHTER

BAMBINA STARTED SNEEZING on 30 October. Then the others started and by next morning Cleo was not eating. I rang Mrs. Philp. She could not see me before the next day, and as it sounded like influenza I was not to bring the cats inside, she would come out to them. In the meantime I gave them homeopathic Aconite and Gelsemium. Bambina took the tablets willingly, Cleo made the most difficulty. At Sharnbrook on 1 November, Mrs. Philp came into our taxi and gave them all injections, "to prevent its turning to pneumonia", followed by tablets. "Clever girl" she said to Bambina as she got one down her, the first. I told her Cleo was not eating. "Then you must force-feed her," she said. "Unless you get liquid food inside her she will get weaker and weaker until she dies. I'll give you a syringe."

"Complan and milk?" I suggested.

"And Brand's Essence of Chicken."

I told the taxi-man to stop at the chemist's in Sharnbrook, where I bought Brand's Essence, and, back home, mixed it with the Complan and milk, slightly warmed. Bambina and Tiutté lapped it, and I filled the syringe and tried to give some to Cleo. Cleo nearly went mad, striking my hands away with her paws. I tried to wrap a towel round her but she was too strong for me. I knelt astride her, but that was worse for she tore my thighs. "Cleo, Cleo, this is to prevent you from dying." It was the biggest battle I have had in my life with a cat, and though I got some down her, I doubted whether it would do her good having been so resisted. She retired to the furthest corner of the room, where she sat hunched and injured, and I medicated my wounds.

In the morning when I came down and opened a tin she came forward and ate. I had feared our relations would not recover, but she was normally friendly.

It was Bambina, this morning, who did not eat. I did not like to force-feed her with the syringe that had been in Cleo's mouth, so opening hers with one hand I tipped some of the mixture into it from a tea-spoon. This way, she took it. She trusted me. She sat on the sofa now, and the basket was abandoned.

I kept the cats in (and had of course warned Stella). On the 3rd I took them back to Mrs. Philp. She was surprised to see them so much better. "They have had a very mild attack. You are fortunate. This will immunise them for three years."

On 10 November Bambina had a relapse and I had to feed her again from the spoon, but on the morning of the 11th she breakfasted.

That afternoon, I planted the little oak-tree. During the summer it had put out whorls of new leaves, but now the sap was sleeping. I turned it from its pot into the hole, and, thinking of the promise I had made it in the dark days at Whitfield Street, said, "Little oak-tree, I have performed."

I thought I had shut Bambina inside, but now could not find her and the light was failing. Instantly anxious, I went about calling, "Bambi, Bambi!" I searched the garden, went out into the Lane and down into the Road. I looked up the dread garden. "Bambi, Bambi!" Perhaps I had overlooked her presence in the house. I went back and searched every room; then went out again and looked in the hen-house and the shed, looked under the vegetation and over the walls. The light was fast going and I was cold with apprehension. I went out and down again to the Road.

And then I saw her: her two white legs like slender columns in the dusk, she faced me from across it. Her back was to a gate to a farmer's field behind the houses on the far side; she must have come from there. Afraid that seeing and dashing towards me she would be hit by a car, I walked towards her with measured steps, crossed, picked her up, and carried her back gripping her tightly. "Darling, you could have died."

I confined her to the kitchen while making sure the cat-flap was closed. After that, I not merely put a tray, I locked her into the kitchen each night before I went to bed. I put a basket in there and a chair, though when I unlocked it in the morning she usually came down from the top of the refrigerator. In the autumn, I turned on the warm-air central heating. The cats loved it and would crouch before the sitting-room outlet, letting it ruffle their hair.

On Christmas Day I shut the cats in, left very early in the morning to go to Tim and his mother, and was back before dark. On 30 December, just before dusk fell, I saw on the lawn something I never thought to see, Tiutté and Cleo playing. It was a good end to the year.

1976 came in with a hurricane, on 2 January. Shutting the cats in, I rushed out and was trying to stake the new trees I had planted when I heard Stella's voice calling to me above the wind that I could be hit by a flying tile. "Come in!"

Tim came up again on the 22nd. The cats were never sure whether they knew him or not. Cleo would turn tail at his approach and hide beneath the shed until he was gone. Bambina and Tiutté were better, but he was staying the night and before dusk I had to ask him to go out for a little whilst I brought them in and gave them their suppers. When he returned they went upstairs; and when he later went upstairs they came down. In the morning, I had to ask him to take a little walk again while I gave them their breakfasts.

On 1 May I missed Bambina again. I searched the house and the garden. I went into the Lane and down to the Road. I crossed and went up into that field. "Bambi, Bambi!" It was still light, but I must get her before dark. At last I brought myself to look into the dread garden, where I had found Cynthia. And there I found her. She was not dead. She was sitting at its far end, beneath the boundary with mine. I tried to send her back into mine, but she dodged and I seized her. I did not want to carry her back towards the Road. There was a broken down shed made of zincs. I climbed with her on to the top of that and then found myself on the Shorts' side of the wall of zincs between their garden – which was sunken – and mine. With Bambina under my left arm, her scruff in my left hand, I pulled myself with my right along the zincs, my feet on the wooden bar to which they were nailed. Then I clutched an elder tree, up and over which I drew myself, and so slid down still holding Bambina, into my own garden. "Oh Bambi, if you knew what anxieties you caused me!"

My legs were cut and scratched. The wire with which I had thought to enclose the garden must be extended – but it was fixed to wooden posts and she climbed those. To cover the wood with something slippery, I took the panels of a plastic compost-bin, put string through the holes and began hanging them over the posts. Then I found the end of the garden full of broken glass. It could cut a cat's feet and I spent more than a day picking it up before I realised it was being thrown in by the children in the farm at the bottom. I went and asked their mother to stop them.

Bambina was with me on my typing-desk when a sparrow lighted on the outside window-sill. She did not try to reach it through the glass. She turned about, to rush through the door from the study into the passage, along the passage into the sitting-room, out through the cat-flap and round to the outside of the window-sill, where she caught it. I took it away from her saying, "My daughter does not kill sparrows," and released it from an upstairs window, but it came to me that what she had done was proof she had in her mind a plan of the house. It was not instinct that had told her she must turn her back on the sparrow to reach it. She had exercised reason.

It was a long time now that I had called her my daughter. Sometimes towards bedtime I would walk with her in my arms, the velvet top of her head beneath my cheek, crooning to her in rhyme:

> Bambina my love,
> Bambina, my dove,
> Treasure,
> Love without measure
> Is thine,
> Daughter of mine,
> Daughter of grace,
> Softer than down
> Beneath my face,
> Safe on my breast,
> Gathered to rest,
> Harlequin clown,
> Caught in my arms,
> Safe from all harms
> — For tears and for laughter —
> Bambina, my daughter.

In the mornings, I always fetched her from the kitchen before I dressed and she came upstairs with me, so exuberant with joy that the stump of her tail wagged. I thought only dogs wagged their tails when happy. Cats twitch or swish them when angry or disturbed. This was not the twitch or swish. It was the vibration of joy that went through the whole of her body, so that the root of her tail vibrated as she purred round me after the long night of separation. As I seated myself cross-legged, I placed her before the holy ones, saying, "Please bless this little one."

26 September was her birthday. "You are two, today!" I told her. "For two years I have preserved you."

I went to find Stella, handed her my camera and asked her to take a picture of Bambina in my arms against the sunflowers that I had nurtured through the drought. Later, I made from it a painting.

WYMINGTON YEARS

WHEN TIM CAME up on 14 October 1976, Bambina, for the first time, rubbed herself against him. Tiutté, though she rose, poised to take flight, decided flight was not needed, and only Cleo flew. When he left, he said, "Bambina behaved beautifully."

On 6 November I fancied she looked not too well, and on the 7th found one of the kitchen gas-taps slightly on. I was appalled that Bambina, shut in the kitchen all night, could have been gassed. She must never sleep in the kitchen again. Though it would mean protecting all my papers at night, she would have to sleep in the study.

On 10 November I noticed that, in the garden, she was squatting rather frequently. I rang Mrs. Philp and asked if she could give me an emergency appointment at her Rushden surgery, at a precise time, as I would have to keep a taxi waiting. "Wait," I said to the driver. Mrs. Philp said, "There is no blockage." If there had been a slight chill, there was no temperature. "No treatment is needed, but I'll give her, now, her booster vaccination." When I emerged with her, the taxi had disappeared. It was a drizzling night, but I thought I would find a phone-box from which I could ring for one, so carrying the basket, I started walking. From Grove Road we passed no phone box. The rain came on more heavily, the weight was slowing me down, and I tried to carry the basket as much as possible under my coat to prevent her from getting further chilled. I must have carried her almost a mile before reaching Little Wymington, where I could place her in the shelter of a phone box whilst I rang for a taxi. After that I changed my taxi firm.

Stella offered to look after my cats if I wanted to stay in London over Christmas, so I went down on the Eve, to Tim's. It was a happy Christmas with him and his mother, but I did think about three little persons, and when I got back, and opened the sitting-room door, they were all standing in a row, waiting for me. They must have heard my key in the latch, "Bless you, darlings!"

January 1977 came in with snow, on the 10th, the first the cats had seen. In the lee of the house I cleared a path for them to a corner where they could relieve themselves, and they kept to it. The hens stayed in their hut. I carried their food up to them in it, and bowls of warmed water.

On 13 March I made a determined attempt to portray Bambina. An earlier attempt, on the scroll-table had not captured her grace; the red lacquer did not offer a sufficient contrast with the tan of her "red" patches; I discarded it and started again on a larger board, placing her on the blue-grey fence. I worked slowly. My easel was now on the landing, but I kept going downstairs to check with the living cat the position of the black and the tan patches . . . the sockets for the whiskers above the eyes . . . the descent of the tan on the right side of her nose, which, as I put it in, I had to be careful did not make the nose look lop-sided. "It's not just a picture, it's a portrait, and I want to show everything exactly as it is." So exactly that, if she were taken from me, I would have this for a record of her as she really was. I worked for three days, and on the 15th wrote in my diary, "Finished the new portrait of Bambina. Very pleased with it." But then, on the 17th, "Worked on Bambina again all day." On the 18th I wrote, "Bambina portrait really finished, I think, this time."

Stella came to tell me Georgius had choked on a fish-bone and died. "Such a big, strong cat, I thought we would have had him for years." I was sorry, too, particularly for Cleo. With the Tiutté family, she was an outsider, but in him she had had a companion. Blueboy, because of an internal trouble, had to be put to sleep, and that left of her kittens only Little Girl; but when they met they humped and hissed at each other. This was most unlike Tiutté and Bambina, who still lay, for preference, touching one another.

On 30 May, Albi died. I would find the white hens died in order of whiteness. I was glad that I had made two paintings of all the eight together. I did not need the eggs of eight hens, but gave some to Tim and took the surplus to the Health Food shop, in Rushden where Mrs. Hawes was amazed by the deep golden orange of their yolks.

On 26 September I wrote in my diary, "Bambina's birthday. Three years old today. Great sense of triumph and relief."

But on 9 October, in a fading light, I noticed she seemed to have a long chin. "Is it really as long as that?" On the following morning there was still that appearance. Was she carrying her lower jaw lower than usual? When I opened the tin, she came forward yet hung back, waiting for the others to eat. I examined her closely, and saw that the right side of her lip and face was swollen. Road burns! I gave her arnica, and opened for her the bottle of Brand's Essence long stored, slightly warmed it, and to my infinite relief she lapped it. By evening she ate a meal. But I wrote in my diary, "Poor little mite, I fear she has been hit by a car again."

The Swiss boys had been posted to Geneva and wanted me to come for a long week-end, and there was a lot of conversation by telephone. I did wish the cats would miaow to them. "Tiutté, try to talk to Tano down the line! See if she can hear you. . . . Bambina has jumped on my desk. . . . Bambi, miaow. . . ." In fact, Bambina very seldom miaowed. For a long time she never miaowed, and when she did it was only a little miaow. The first time I heard it was in the study, and I exclaimed in delight, "You spoke!"

On 14 October I flew from Gatwick . . . and then they were running to me with open arms. They had taken a room for me in a hotel, but I would have my meals with them in Tano's flat. Jean-Louis had a flat in another street but came to Tano each evening to eat, as it was Tano who did the cooking. The huge photograph of Greta Garbo against the red silk still dominated the room. . . . It was near the Jet d'Eau, and when we walked down to the lake the lights were playing through the sparklets of water. Next day they took me on a pleasure-steamer from which new vistas unrolled. Jean-Louis said, "Our friendship began with cats. . . ." I arrived back on the 17th at about 9.00 in the evening, and I must have been very tired for I wrote in my diary only, "Cats all well." But I see that I wrote it twice.

On 9 December as I was shutting the door from the sitting-room into the garden I felt it stick and gave it a pull. I had caught in it a hen's foot. It was poor Speck. I gave her an Arnica tablet and smeared the foot with Arnica ointment; though horny, it was obviously sensitive and she stood holding it in the air.

Then I could not see Bambina. I was having a driving lesson at 3.00 and must get her in before I left as before I got back it would be dark. I ran out, calling everywhere. I stopped for a moment before the dread garden and, pressed for time, darted in without asking permission and was upbraided by the emerging owner. "I'm looking for my cat," I said. "It was in your garden I found her sister, dead." Stella had told me other cats had been found dead there. It was a danger-spot because there was no railing dividing it from the very narrow pavement, but a hedge so that a motorist would not see a cat coming out in sufficient time to slow. . . . Bambina was not there. I found and confined her in safety just before my bell rang. My instructor, Graham Inwood, to whom I told the story, must have seen that I was still trembling, for he took me, instead of through streets, through the leafy lanes of Yielden, and said, "Promise me, when you have passed your test, never to drive when upset."

As always, I spent Christmas with Tim. When I returned, Bambina was so thankful to see me it was almost distressing. She licked my face and accompanied me everywhere from room to room.

It was on 14 February, 1978, I noticed Bambina was sometimes afraid of the hens. They were bigger than she was, and, clustered round the garden-door, could prevent her from going out. I picked her up and carried her over their heads.

On 29 May, Jenny died. I tried to moisten her beak but the life had gone and I buried her. I was sorry for Polly. They had always walked together, staying up later than the white hens. Now Polly, still staying up later, walked alone, and I wondered if she felt that the one who had always walked at her side walked at her side no longer.

My hens were down to four: Polly, Susan, Dulcie and Speck, still a little lame.

I finished my *Bacon*, and on 21 August cleared a space on the floor of my study and set out three copies for pagination. I heard a scratching at the door. It was Bambina. I was afraid of a cat's muddling the pages, yet did not like to rebuff her. "If I let you in while I am doing this, could you be very good and quiet and not catch at the pages?"

It was as if she had understood me, for she sat in my lap watching the pages turn and my pencil mark them, yet never attempting to seize by mouth or paw: sat sweet and good, though the process was long. "You know this is serious for me."

One episode I cannot date from my diary. It was during the season over which the B.B.C. presented all the plays of Shakespeare. I watched them all, except that I missed *The Comedy of Errors* on Christmas Eve at Tim's. It was being repeated in the summer. Hardly had it begun than I noticed Bambina was missing. I ran out, calling, "Bambi! Bambi!" I had to go into the Lane and round to the back, up into the dread garden. . . . Though it was near to midsummer, the light was going, when, in the farmer's field behind the gate where I had found her long ago, I discerned at the furthest edge a little white figure running, running. She was running after rabbits. I called her and she came. I gathered her into my arms and carried her back to the house just as *The Comedy of Errors* was ending.

In the autumn of 1978 I did a lot of painting. The last time I had submitted anything to Chelsea they had preferred one of my Sherwood landscapes, *Excavation at Dawn*. This year they hung my *Hens Drinking* — all the eight of them — and, though having just finished the *Bacon* I was doing some illustrations for it, that gave me the impetus before starting on *Saint-Germain*, to go on and do further hen-paintings.

1979 brought the heaviest fall of snow I had known. Starting on 15 February, it piled up several feet deep, and working from breakfast time it took me until 4.00 p.m. to cut a path to the hen house. The hens came out on to it, and I brought them water I had heated in a kettle. They drank it appreciatively and ate the corn I brought them before the light went.

The cats bore up but were not well; Tim told me on the phone that Dizzy was never well when there was snow. There was one bonus. I had found Cleo difficult to paint outside because her colouring merged into the vegetation. Against the snow she showed up, which was perhaps part of the reason why she disliked it. She hunched almost into a ball. Despite it, I noted two days later that all four hens were laying and that Polly had made a friend of Dulcie. I do not think Dulcie ever took the place of Jenny for her, but she walked now with Dulcie, and Susan walked with Speck.

On 12 June, I noted Speck was very weak. On the next day I had to help her into the hen-house, and on 14 June she died. I buried her beneath the purple Louis Spathe lilac I had planted.

Bambina on her fifth birthday was graceful and lovely, and it was a good period for my paintings of her: frolicking on the lawn, stretched casually on the carpet, or perched on the medals cabinet, erected tall, or casually, one leg hanging over.

On 2 October Dulcie died, and on the following day I noted, "Polly very poorly." On 5 December she looked so chilled I brought her in to warm. But Susan laid, on the shortest day, 21 December.

Christmas was off for that year. Tim's mother was gravely ill and he was sharing with her the dinner served in the hospital. So it was that I was at home when, on the morning of Christmas Day, there was a rat-tat-tat on the door telling me Susan wanted to come in; and she laid me an egg, in the big arm-chair, on the morning of Christmas Day.

Moreover she celebrated the new year, 1980, by laying on 1 January and 2 January. Then she rested. She was six years old and I gave her nourishing food to sustain her through her moult.

For Tim it was a year of bereavement. On 23 February he telephoned to tell me his mother had died in the night. Six months later his cat died.

I had been working for some time on a series of portraits of Cleo, posed on the black Chinese what-not — usually with eggs, casually placed there, looking as though she was hatching them and which she never broke — and on 28 February finished the last one: poised to spring down.

On 29 March, Susan came out of her moult and laid again, and on 30 March, to my surprise, Polly laid again, just one egg. Susan's laying became again regular, but by 16 May Polly was ill. In the evening I looked for her to carry her to the hen-house, but found she had crept into the bathroom, where she lay. There was blood on the floor. I fetched Stella. She said, "The end is near. There is nothing you can do for her except make her comfortable." So I made a bed of soft materials beneath her, in the spot she had chosen, and put a bowl of water by it, for her, though she was past taking it. Her breathing was becoming less. "Please God take her, she is in pain." In the morning I had to go to London. When I returned, she was dead. I carried her out, and in the evening light buried her amongst the tulips.

Susan was now my only hen. Throughout the summer, benefiting from the whole of the attention she had shared with the others, she developed enormously in intelligence and character. She followed me everywhere, and I took photographs of her on the arm of the sofa, stretching up to take butter from the table, sharing a saucer with Bambina or a plate with all of the cats. She was bigger than they, so pushed in between them. Stella photographed her eating from my hand. She laid right through the autumn until 8 November, when again she rested and moulted. I did not know her exact age, but thought she must be well into her seventh year if not indeed seven. I kept her in all day, though as the daylight faded she still showed a will to return to the hen-house for the night, which I respected.

On 23 December 1980 I passed my driving test. I went down by public transport on the morrow to spend Christmas with Tim — this was the first year there were just the two of us — and when I returned on Boxing Day, Graham delivered my bright red Fiat 127, LWL 707S, "Robin," an object of immense pride and delight to me; the cats swarmed all over it.

On 5 February, 1981, I noted in my diary: "Susan's comb reddening. She will lay again soon. She walks around looking for a suitable box. Have provided one which has just come in."

I finished the main portrait of Cleo on 20 April. Cleo and Tiutté were due for re-vaccination and I asked Mrs. Philp to come and do it at the house. They disappeared under the furniture, and had to be recovered. "If you had brought them to my surgery they would have sat still."

"Paralysed with fright?" I suggested.

"Nicely paralysed." She was giving up practice. This concerned me as I did not know of another vet in Rushden.

Susan laid until 13 May, when she went off again. On 13 June I noted, "Susan showing her age. Has even difficulty in managing the step." On 14 June I wrote, "Susan failing, begins to stand with her eyes closed. Comb has gone right down, flopped." Yet on 11 July, I recorded with joy, "Susan is recovering. Her comb is red again and her steps more sprightly."

It was about this time that she found for herself a compartment of the kitchen cupboard that suited her to sleep in. It was empty, and when I saw how perfectly it fitted her I had not the heart to fill it again with tins. It became Susan's cupboard. I placed a fresh newspaper in it each day, and was always down in good time to let her out. She had become a house-hen, who pecked about the garden by day but came in for the night.

On 24 July Susan laid what was to be her last egg. She had become very dear to me, and I would not get new hens while she lived, for they would upset her. I did without eggs.

Chelsea took two of my pictures that year, *Bambina Yawning* and another of the *Hens Drinking*, both marked NOT FOR SALE of course as always.

Freed from having to take driving lessons, I was taking riding lessons with Shirley Warner up the road and piano lessons with Richard Wilkinson, the latter because I felt I must be able to play at least a little of the music of *Saint-Germain*. It was on 9 November, after I had had a piano lesson from 1-2 that I reckoned I had time to drive into Bedford for something. It took longer than I had thought and on the road back the light was going. I worried about Susan and I trod on the accelerator. With no one to open the door to the sitting-room for her, I supposed she would go to the hen-house, but to my dismay she was simply standing, motionless, out in the garden, in the cold, sheltered only by the two flower-pots between which she had placed herself.

I ran to her. She was frozen.

I brought her into the house, made a hot water-bottle and laid her on it, and tried to get her circulation going, but though it improved a little on her right, her left foot and left side seemed not to work.

In the morning of the 10th I offered her some of the cats' Whiskas, which she always liked as a treat. She did not eat, but turned round within her cupboard to face the wall. She stayed there all day.

Throughout the 11th it was the same. She ate nothing, took no water.

On the 12th, I felt she would die unless I could get something down her. I mixed milk, Complan and egg-yolk and fed this from a syringe into her beak. She must have recovered a little of her strength for afterwards she ate some of the Whiskas liver, Whiskas tuna and some crumbled wholemeal bread. Yet she could only drag herself, on one side, not stand.

On 13 November, in the morning, she did not open her beak to eat. I made the same mixture as before and tried to inject it into her mouth from the syringe. Suddenly there was a convulsion, and she was dead in my arms.

Had I been wrong to force-feed? Infinitely distressed, I dug a grave for her, near to the house, beside the "little" cyprus-trees the Swiss boys had given me, which was now grown big. As I lowered her into the grave, I prayed to the Masters of Wisdom, "Please let her individuality be preserved. I could not bear her to be reborn as a battery hen. Unless she can come back to me, reincarnated as a hen in my care, let her rest in my arms, in my bosom."

On 14 December, Bambina was not well, vomited, and in the morning, though she ate, sat continually over her water-bowl. A Scot, Allan Adams, had set up a veterinary practice in Rushden; I telephoned him for an appointment. It was not, as I feared, a kidney failure, but an infection of the bowel. He gave her something and next day she was better. Yet in the evening of 7 January, 1982, she was sitting over her water-bowl again. I gave her Aconite 30, and before I went to bed she rose, suddenly, and ate. The snow descended next day. Perhaps it was only its imminence that had disturbed her.

I now transferred Bambina's sleeping quarters from the study to the large upstairs bedroom beside mine. This made it easier to bring her into mine as soon as I rose and seated myself for meditation, which ended always in the same prayer for her.

Cleo lost her what-not when it had to go upstairs to make room for the piano I bought; but by running up and down the keys produced strange music.

I bought no more hens for some time, but on 10 June I motored to Raunds and brought eight Black Rockets back in my car. They had been kept in rows, and when liberated into the hen-house at first stood in a row facing the end wall. If I picked one up and set it outside, it went straight back into the line. It was not until 13 June that, as the light was going, they took their first timid steps outside. They were handsome, with gold speckled breasts and scolloped collars, and, in some, a slight sheen of green on the back. I named them Marigold, Hannah, Dot, Emerald, Esmerelda, Jet, Sooty and Blackie. They now became destructive, and on 18 June chased all of my cats. I therefore confined them within the run except for supervised outings.

On 17 October suddenly Cleo and Tiutté were fighting across my desk and typewriter. I said, "Stop it! Peace!" The next day Cleo ran away from me and was afraid to eat with the other cats. On the 19th she was no better and I took her to Allan Adams. He asked, "Has a dog bitten her?"

"I don't think so." Then I remembered the fight with Tiutté.

That Christmas, 1982, on the Eve, I drove all the way to Tim's flat in St. John's Wood. When I got back on Boxing Day, Bambina was so pathetically glad to see me, jumping up and licking my face, that when I told Tim on the phone he agreed to my bringing her, too, next year.

The little oak-tree concerned me now. In Whitfield Street I thought in terms of planting it out when I had a garden, but it was spreading out faster than I had expected and one branch was so far over the patio that it would be in at my window soon. I must find it some wider space. Irchester Country Park? Or at Shirley's? After having ridden for a year, jumped, galloped and fallen off five times, I had stopped, but there remained between us a friendship. On 5 June 1983, I asked her. She consulted with her husband and then told me, "We should love to have the little oak-tree." It could not be moved while in full leaf, but in the autumn. "We hope you will come and talk to it sometimes," she said. I talked to it now, telling it not to put out too much further growth this year, as a big shock was going to come to it in its transplantation, though this was to allow it its fullest development. I showed it the painting I had made of the great oak in Sherwood, as a model of what it could become, and said, "You have to have the space." On 20 August we celebrated the 21st anniversary of my mother's having picked it up as an acorn.

19 November had been fixed as the day for the transplantation and as it approached I could hardly bear it. The leaves had turned to golden and red. The glory

seemed to be crying. I was so afraid it would die. I got out my paints, and the pain of parting was in the painting I made of it, through the reds, in the autumn mists.

Bob came with their two big sons and they dug and dug. The earth fell away, leaving a pitiful root bare as they heaved it on to the tractor. I rode with it, in the fading light. They had chosen the site with care, at not quite the top of a hill, so that its back would be protected from the north wind and yet it would face the sun all day. But had they taken enough root? I prayed for it all the time, and went back and prayed for it the next day and for many days after that. I commended it to all the Masters of Wisdom and asked each one of them to preserve it, for my mother's sake and for its own.

Back in the garden there was the immense gaping hole. I motored to Podington Nurseries to ask for a pool to be installed in the hole. To put in goldfish I would have to wait till the spring.

I carried up Maxicrop in which to bathe the twigs of the oak-tree, and believed it had a new bud that was green. "I have so many children, children with fur, children with feathers, children with leaves. You will outlive Bambina, you will outlive me. But perhaps I shall find my way back to you in another incarnation. Perhaps we shall all meet again under your boughs."

On 24 December I packed Bambina into her basket. I did not care to drive with her beside me, and so hired a taxi so that I could hold the basket on my knee and tell her, through the little window, "This is so that we shall not be separated at Christmas."

When I opened it in Tim's flat she was terrified and ran straight under the divan-bed. We had to leave her there. He set a tray for her in the bathroom, and food, but both remained untouched. "Perhaps she'll come out when I leave," said Tim as he cleared away our evening meal.

Sure enough, after he had closed the door and I had put out the light, a sudden plonk told me she was no longer under the bed but on top of it. And there she stayed, licking my face, kneading me. "Darling, darling . . . you are happy now, you know that you are safe, but this is the time for going to sleep." I reached up and stroked her as she lay on my breast, but she was too excited to settle and the kneading and licking went on hour after hour. I felt I should try to obtain a little sleep before the dawn and carried her into the bathroom, where I made up a bed for her with soft things on the floor — and felt mean as I shut the door, leaving her scratching to get back to me.

It was Tim who discovered her when he went to the bathroom on Christmas morning, and she bolted straight back under the divan.

While Tim was doing the cooking I managed to coax her out and gathered her into my arms. "Have a look round you." She was quiet until I re-introduced her to Tim. He took a step towards us, as if to stroke her, but she flinched violently. "It's your cigarette. She's frightened of the smoke." He consigned it to an ash-tray and tried again. But she turned her face away from him and tried to creep up behind my neck to hide hers.

"It's me," he lamented. "It's not the flat, it's not the cigarette, it's me."

"Darling, you have met Tim before . . . you have rubbed yourself against him." But I had to let her go back beneath the divan. On the morning of Boxing Day she appeared, for the first time, in the front sitting-room, where we were having breakfast. We both kept very quiet, not to frighten her. She hesitated in, then crept under the couch. "She is taking courage," I said. "She is exploring. If she were here for a few days she would be all right."

"I can't say I blame her," he said. "To be picked up from one's home and carried to a place one doesn't know must be horrid. I can't think of anything nastier." But, as the hour for my taxi to come approached he advised me, "Get her. She'll jump when she hears the bell, and if she goes under the bed again it will be difficult to get her out."

Surveying her for the last time in my arms, before she went into the basket, he said, "You could have had a much nicer Christmas."

Back at Wymington, when I opened the basket and she saw that she was in her own sitting-room, she climbed out and became immediately normal. I told Tiutté and Cleo we were back and then went up to tell the little oak-tree.

My empty pool still gaped. On 25 April, 1984, I went back to Podington. It was still too early for fish, but I brought back pond-plants. On 30 April, at last I obtained two goldfish. They were Comets, with long tails, and I took only two so that I could get to know them as individuals. One had a longer tail, with more white on it, than the other. Mr. Reed could not tell me their sex, so I called them Flo and Rho, which could stand for either Floris or Florence and Rhodophis or Rhoda. When I liberated them into the pool they went straight to the bottom and hid under the weeds. Next morning revealed them alive but still hiding.

The literature said one should not change the water; that cloudiness would settle and clear. This did not happen. It grew thicker and I saw Flo and Rho only when they came up to feed — for they did become tamer. In the winter, they went to the bottom to hibernate.

This Christmas Tim and I agreed Bambina should be left at home.

On 1 January 1985, the Swiss boys telephoned. On the tenth anniversary of their leaving England they thought to come again; perhaps for my birthday, on 7 March. Tim always came for my birthday, but when I told him this he said, "Tell them I'll cook for everybody."

It was, however, on Friday 5th April they came. I was at Bedford railway station to meet them, and led them to my car. As I drove them, Jean-Louis said, "Will Tiutté remember Tano?"

When I brought them into the sitting-room, all the cats disappeared into hiding. "Where is Tiutté?" asked Jean-Louis.

"Under the sofa."

"Of course!" said Tano, gently mocking, ear-to-ear smiling, and went down on his knees to try to see her, but she would not come out.

They found their old rooms and rejoiced to see that the tiny cyprus-tree they had had at Whitfield Street was now of immense girth and towered above our heads. They were perplexed by my concern to get Bambina in before dark and take her upstairs, separating her from the others. "She would not go out?" queried Jean-Louis. "Not out of the garden?"

Flo and Rho had emerged from their hibernation, and the next morning I took the boys to see the little oak-tree.

It was not until late evening of that second day that Tiutté emerged from under the sofa. She came forward very slowly, and stood in the middle of the room, looking very hard at Tano. We all kept quiet and still, for we felt what was ticking in her brain, stirring in her memory. She looked and looked, and at last walked straight foward, straight to him, and rubbed herself against him.

Softly we all applauded. "Tiutté remembers Tano. After ten years! It is a long time in the life of a cat." She weaved around his legs and he was able to stroke and pat her.

Tano made our Sunday dinner. They opened the champagne they had brought and Tano said, "To our friendship!"

On Monday I drove them back to Bedford.

I had tired of waiting for the water in the pool to clear and on 7 May baled it out with a bowl and refilled from the hose, using Haleox. At last I could see Flo and Rho again. After this I changed the water almost weekly and they were always much enlivened thereby, coming up to feed immediately. They grew, and were destined to grow to seven or eight inches.

In September I had to go to France for a few days. From Compiègne on the 21st I glimpsed the new moon. I wanted to wish on it for the three new books I had in the pipe-line, *Saint-Germain, Blavatsky* and *Déricourt*, but all I could say was, "Please, may I find Bambina safe when I get home." I was back for her eleventh birthday.

On 7 November I saw a card advertising four Rhodes Red pullets on point of lay and two Rhodes Red–Light Sussex cross chicks of eight weeks. Though I still had Black Rockets, I had always wanted to own one of the ancient, pure breeds, so went to see them. In a run in a back-garden I was shown the birds: two dark red and two golden red. The man said, "They're all pure bred; I don't know why there's a difference in colour." I said I would buy them, but what I fell in love with were the two chicks, which walked everywhere side by side. I had not meant to have chickens in case the cats killed them, but the man said there were cats around his place. "The chicks keep with the big hens, who chase the cats away." So the four big hens were packed into a big box and the two copper-coloured chicks into the two compartments of a small one, and loaded on to my car.

I waited till dusk, then dragged the big box into the run and opened it. The first who stepped out was the fairest. She looked so lovely that I exclaimed, "Oh Diana!" The next to follow was the deeper golden: "Phoebe!" Then came the two dark reds, which I named after heroines with red hair: Silvia and Anne Shirley. They walked in pairs, the two blondes side by side and the two redheads; perhaps they were pairs of sisters.

When I opened the wooden box to let out the chicks, it seemed to me one was worse affected than the other. She kept going, "Cheep! Cheep!" in a distressed way that worried me, as I put them into the hen-house with the others.

When I came down in the morning the Black Rockets and Rhodes Reds were out, the blacks as the established residents pecking the reds a bit but not too badly, and one chick was running about. Where was the other? She was not in the hut; not in the crevice at the back; if she had got out, she was not under the elder or the shed. I searched for hours. The one who was running about was silent. It was little "Cheep! Cheep!" who was gone. At 3.45 I saw a cat, not one of my cats, but a tabby owned by people at the back, making for the remaining chick. I rushed forward to save her and was only just in time. Now I knew what had happened to "Cheep! Cheep!" and in the same moment I saw the remains of her feathers. Carrying the surviving chick in my arms, I made for the house. In the sitting-room were Bambina, Tiutté and Cleo. "I can't put you down here."

I took her into the bathroom, closed the door and set her down. "You will have to live there, until you are old enough not to be killed by a cat." There was a mat for her to sit on, and I brought in bowls of corn and water. I looked in on her last thing before the light went.

Next morning when I came down she was not on the mat. She was so small, she had crept into the crevice between the wash-basin pedestal and the wall. Though she must have felt safer so protected, she was on cold linoleum, so I lined the crevice with newspaper.

Outside, the Reds had followed the Blacks into the shed at dusk, and this morning they had come out as one flock.

After the Swiss boys had left, I had reflected that they were probably right about Bambina. She was so much older, now, that she no longer went beyond the garden and I should let her sleep with the other cats, below. When I came down in the mornings I first greeted the cats, waiting for me in the sitting-room, went with them into the kitchen and opened a tin, looked into the bathroom to see how the chick had weathered the night and then went out to feed and water the hens before making my own breakfast. But some days later, when I came down in the morning, I was horrified to see the chick standing in the sitting-room. She was facing the three cats, who were all standing in a line, looking at her. Incredibly, the chick was standing her tiny ground. I opened a tin of cat-food in the kitchen. The chick walked forward and pecked, with the cats, from their plates. They withdrew a little. Suddenly I wondered if she was Susan, and if the cats gave way to her because they remembered her as she had been when she was so much larger.

Later in the morning I carried her out and set her on the lawn, to walk a little under my supervision. I had been calling her all this time "the chick". What should her name be? Rhodes was in the eastern Mediterranean, and I do not know why I thought of the island of Delos, but it came to me in the quiet, her name was Delia.

I took her out for some part of each day, walked her in the sun and watched her pick up worms. "Your only duty is to grow," I told her. One worm, I thought, was too big for her to get down, but, though with difficulty, she managed it.

For Christmas, I decided to spread the bathroom with newspaper and put corn and water so that it would not be necessary to let her out when coming in to feed the cats, and she was well on my return.

The year's turn brought snow. On 1 January, 1986, I wrote, "Delia out for only half an hour. Seemed to feel the cold cruelly. Yet the cats are afraid of her beak," on the 2nd, "Delia out for a respectable time, on the 3rd, "Snow gone," on the 4th, "Delia out for a little longer, picking up worms again," and on the 23rd, "Delia actually stepped out into the garden on her own, a change from having to be put out."

On the 25th there was a gleam of sun on the lawn and I let the big hens out, so that they could walk down grass touched to a golden green. I went back into the house, and when I looked out again there was something dark in the goldfish pool. Puzzled, I hurried out. It was a hen, floating, all save her head, which was beneath the water. It was handsome Hannah. She was dead. Even in death it could be seen she was in the peak of condition. Her comb was red and full for she had just come on to lay. She must have lent forward to drink and lost her balance. She would have tried to climb out, but the plastic sides of the pool offered no foothold, and her feathers, filled with water, made her body heavy.

Flo and Rho were unharmed, but the next day I went to Podington to buy plastic netting to place over the pool.

Delia prospered and grew. She explored, investigated everything. It was perhaps the period during which she gave greatest delight. With a flutter and spring she was on my typing-stool. In another moment she had one foot on the typewriter. I photographed her "typing". She found the staircase, but the steps were too steep for her to go one leg after the other and she had to do a flutter and spring to mount each one. Yet she reached the upper floor and my bedroom. I feared her spoiling it and guided her downwards. Going downstairs was also difficult for her. Although she was not big, there did not seem enough in front of her to land on, and she had, at each stair, to turn a little sideways.

The snow came back in the first week of February, and on the 8th when a handyman called I passed him my camera and asked him to take photographs of us both together. He took three, one of me with Delia on the wrist of my outstretched arm like a little falcon posed to take flight; one of her on my shoulder and one with her almost on the back of my neck, all against a background of snow.

From a painter's point of view she was under the same disadvantage as Cleo. Her copper plumage did not show up well against the vegetation, but the snow gave me an opportunity, and I made the painting that captures the memory of her as she was then: the trim figure rising from the slender column of her legs, like two sides of a vase with answering curves of breast and rump, and small, finely poised head.

I had to call the plumber, and it surprised him to find a chicken in the sitting-room, especially with cats. "Wait," I said, "while I open a tin." Now that Delia shared their meals I could never serve them chicken, but I opened a tin of Whiskas Rabbit. "The plumber gasped, "The chicken's coming, too!" He gaped as the three cats and Delia gathered round the plate to eat, and said, "Well now I've seen everything. Just wait till I get home to tell my children what I've seen today!"

Did Delia think she was a cat? She showed some interest in the big hens, walking up to the hen-run, looking at them through the wire. More than once, I introduced her, for a few minutes, under my supervision, but each time, they attacked her so cruelly that she was no sooner in than desperate to get out and I had to rescue her. "My poor dear, you are humanised and felinised."

I still never left her outside alone; I would not till she was full grown. She was indeed growing. She could no longer squeeze her body into the crevice between the washstand pedestal and the wall. For some time she still put her head in it. Then one morning I found her on the inside sill of the window, above the bath. It was tiled and must be cold to her feet, so after that I always folded newspaper and laid it on the sill each evening before she retired.

Her comb was beginning to rise and to become red, and on 28 March, Good Friday, I missed her. Then I saw that the door of the linen-cupboard was a-jar. I opened it and she was there. She had laid her first egg, on the linen. It was a beautiful copper-brown, like her plumage, soft as silk beneath my cheek.

Now that she was full-grown, I no longer feared her being out in the garden alone. When the weather warmed, I left therefore, the window of the bathroom open at night, so that at first light she could let herself out. It was quite a drop, down to the patio, and she did a lot of looking before she first trusted herself to her wings; then she spread them and, partially air-borne, flutter-jumped down, landing not directly beneath the window but almost five feet from it.

Outside, Diana had learned how to jump on to the top of the gate of the run and thence down into the garden, followed by Phoebe, Silvia and Anne. I thrilled with admiration, but the damage they did the garden was too great and, feeling rather mean, I put netting over the top of the run. I still let them out for supervised runs, but Delia was the only one free all the time. She laid her eggs precariously, on the bathroom sill and I was always expecting one to roll down into the bath.

The cats enjoyed the summer. They found large saucers for flower-pots in which they curled themselves. But at home, on the sofa, Bambina and Tiutté liked to lie touching each other. The bond of consanguinity was not broken.

Ever since Delia had learned to let herself out, I had wondered if she could learn to let herself in. To jump up would be much more difficult than jumping down, and in the evening she would always come to the door to the sitting-room, asking to be let in. If I was not there, she would stand waiting for me. I must show her there was a direct way. She liked being picked up and would crouch as an invitation. I picked her up from the patio and held her up to the sill of the open bathroom window, showing her that from my hands she could step on to it, and find herself from whence she had sprung down in the morning. I showed her this a number of times, gradually lowering the height to which I raised her. Then I put the garden chair in front of the window. She tried, from the seat, but the back of it got in the way. I must try to find a large wooden box. . . .

On 7 June I was in the bathroom when, to my utter delight, Delia flew in at the window.

"You have achieved! You can get back into your home. Now you can let yourself both out and in."

It was a great relief to me, because it meant that when winter came, if I had to be out in the afternoon, I would not have to choose between bringing Delia in before I went, while it was still light, and worrying about whether I was going to be back in time to let her in before dusk.

On 22 July, Bambina was off her food. She lay in the long grass all day, and in the evening I took her to Allan Adams. She was seen by one of his assistant vets. He gave her something, but then asked, "How did she lose her teeth?"

"Lose her teeth?"

"She should have two canines coming up from below to meet the two from above."

I had never noticed. "I did not see them come out."

"Born like that?"

When I got home I checked with the portrait *Bambina Yawning*, which I made in February 1980. Sure enough, I had depicted two fine little white teeth descending, but none in her lower jaw. Yet a car had pitched her on to her face. . . .

On 28 August Tiutté was unwell. Allan Adams said she had an enlarged liver. But he gave her something, and next day she was better. On 13 September it was Bambina who was unwell. I feared she had cat flu. Adams assured me she had not, gave her something and next day she was normal.

On 26 September, Bambina's twelfth birthday, I opened the door from the sitting-room to the garden in the morning to find her posed just outside on the white polyurethene "drum" (which floated pebbles to enable the fish to breathe when the pool iced over). The light was partly behind her and creeping round the edges of her fur gave her a look that was almost fey. I took photographs and later made them into a painting.

It was later that day that Marigold died. There remained of the Black Rockets only the two Blackies and Dot, whom I foresaw would be the survivor.

It was on 6 October, 1986, between 5.30 and 5.45, when I opened the door to the garden to call Bambina in for her "tea", that I found her just outside, but wrinkling her lip at something beyond it. To see what it was, I opened it wider and saw a ginger kitten. As he crossed the threshold I called him Alexander. He saw Tiutté and Cleo eating and went to join them, Bambina following. When he had eaten, he went out again. I rang Tim, to tell him. "He's rather nice."

"I should have him."

It was what I was thinking of doing. His calls became regular. When Tim came for his birthday on 15 October, Alexander walked down the path. "Hullo, ginger," Tim greeted him. To me, he said, "This is my favourite colour."

He did not upset my cats, or Delia — on 17 October I wrote, "Delia is the only hen still laying, and daily, too, still big, brown full-sized eggs." From his being so thin, he must be a stray. On the 18th he did not come in, or on the 19th. On the 20th he reappeared, but with most of his whiskers broken off or browned and curled at the ends. I telephoned Allan Adams for an appointment on the 23rd, and kept him in until it. As he stepped from the basket loudly purring Adams' assistant vet said, "He's obviously very healthy and very happy but his whiskers have been burned off." I could only think he had tried to take food that was cooking. On the vaccination certificate I saw his age estimated at seven months.

For some days I took him out only on collar and lead, and in case he slipped away, attached to the collar a cylinder with my name and address in it. On the 29th I let him out for the first time without the lead, and in the doorway he crossed with Bambina, a sign that each had accepted the other. But he went straight to the goldfish pool and I was glad the netting protected Flo and Rho.

I wanted him to learn to use the cat-flap, but for a long time he just miaowed outside or came in through the bathroom window, which had to be open for Delia. When I saw ginger streak across the garden twice, I suspected he must have a twin. On 5 November, Ken brought me back the collar and cylinder. "This dropped off in our garden." For some time, he said, the ginger stray had haunted the back of their house. He had advised Stella, "Don't bring him inside," but she put food outside for him, "Then he disappeared."

"I'm sorry. I wouldn't have taken a cat. . . ."

"It's the best thing that could have happened," he said. Then he added, "Have you seen that other cat, like him?"

"I may have done. I wasn't sure if it was another."

"There are two of them. We call the other Doppelgänger." He did not want Doppelgänger, either.

Alexander had white shirt-front and paws, but Döppelganger was ginger all over. I called him Edward, but though they were obviously twins, he was too timid to come forward.

Tiutté now resented Alexander, and would sometimes growl at him for no reason as he lay on the sofa. One morning, while I was feeding them, backing away from him she jumped up on to a drawer that happened to be open. I picked up her plate of food and served it to her up there. After this, I always did that. She would jump up on to the drawer to wait for it, and became again a happier cat.

The shortening days brought a problem . . . I took my bath about 5.30. In the summer, this was before Delia came in. Now, she was already roosted on the sill. I closed the window and had my bath beneath her. The rising steam fidgeted her, but she got used to it, and I afterwards opened the window again to let the steam out. Yet would she not now feel the cold, being so much more exposed than the hens in the hut? If I closed the window she would be unable to let herself out at first light. I nailed a curtain three-quarters of the way across the lower part of the window-frame, so that it protected her, and yet she could get out in the morning.

Alexander still used this "door" and seemed not to disturb Delia, but from the bathroom into the rest of the house there was no way unless I left internal doors open. . . . On 25 November, at last, he used the cat-flap. That meant that I was able to close all the doors when I left on Christmas Eve, and when I returned on Boxing Day I found all well.

On 12 January 1987 the big freeze began. As soon as Delia had flown in I closed the window behind her and she could not go out until I came down in the morning. The water in the pool froze and, as the polyurethane drum meant to enable the goldfish to breathe had been shredded and eaten by the Black Rockets, I had each morning to carry out kettles of boiling water to melt the ice. It was, however, the cats who suffered most. For their sakes I left the central heating on all night, and put trays for them inside. In the day-time I would see them picking their way along the path I had cleared, to dig their holes in the snow. On the 20th the thaw came, but Bambina looked poorly and on 2 February I took her to Allan Adams. I said, "She has gone very thin, and her coat is not as glossy as it used to be."

He found nothing wrong with her, but said, "I'll give her an injection of anabolic steroids. They should build her up and put more muscle and weight on her."

"Now you will run and jump again," I told her.

But on 26 February I wrote, "Cats have been off food for some time. On advice from Leslie Linnell (who served in the shop) gave them Princes sardines in oil. They fell on it." I also bought fresh plaice and steamed it. This was chiefly for Bambina, though the others had some, too.

One thing I was sorry about. Bambina now tended to give way to Alexander, and at feeding-time hung back behind him and Cleo. I would not have had this happen for the world, and sometimes I carried her upstairs by herself so that she would walk about on me and knead me with her paws as she used to do. "You are my baby, my darling, my daughter."

It was in the garden when the crocuses had come out round the pool that I snapped Alexander and Edward attempting to fish, and later made a painting from the picture. Alexander was the most persistent attempting fisher. He had, also, now learned to stand up on his hind legs, for moments without support, and I applauded him, "Mummy's little man!" It was, however, with Edward that Bambina formed a friendship.

On 4 May I recorded, "The end of poor Blackie. Dot is now the sole survivor of the Black Rockets."

On 23 May in the evening I did not find Delia on the bathroom window-sill. I went out in the garden calling, "Delia! Delia!" I searched every room in the house. Then I found her. She was in Susan's old cupboard. It gave me a turn.

I did not encourage her to sleep there, because from the kitchen she could not let herself out and in.

On 15 June Alexander led Edward in for his "tea" and sat back while he ate.

It was on 4 July I read in *The Cat* Mrs. Earnshaw had died. Her good deeds must bring her good karma. I wrote an appreciation of her to the editor, Group Captain Boothby.

26 September was Bambina's thirteenth birthday. I wanted a good birthday picture of her, but though she posed on the sill in the sun I saw with sadness that her coat was more open than when she had been in her prime. It was no longer glossy. She looked a little ragged, a little tired, and rather thin.

Tiutté had gone very thin. Tim noticed it when he came on 15 October.

Lesley's husband wanted to be rid of their chickens so she brought them all to me, saying, "Perhaps I could come and see them sometimes?" But one was a cock and I protested, "If he mates my hens their eggs will become fertile. I shan't want to eat eggs that could become chicks and if I let them hatch the cats will get them."

"It's not the mating season," she said.

I would have to find someone else to take the cock before the spring. . . . On 7 November, when I had let them all out for a run, from the house I saw Rupert had Delia by the back of the neck. I thought he was maltreating her and rushed out. He was mating her.

"Oh Delia! Are you going to become a mother?"

On 18 November I had lunch with a publisher in London; I would return by the 3.20 bus so, as I would not be home till after dark, I took special care with the arrangements for Delia. I made sure the curtain of the bathroom window was pinned back in exactly the right way, so that it would not flap in her face as she came in, and I turned on the bathroom light, so that she would see it beckoning. It must have been 5.30 when the return bus put me down at Wymington Turn and I started to walk down the hill. I had been becoming anxious, and my anxiety increased. Seized by foreboding, I began to run, my coat flapping in the wind holding me back. "Delia, I am coming!" I called aloud, as I panted along, stumbling. At last I got into the house. Delia was not on the inside bathroom sill. The folded paper was there, as I had left it, unused.

Why had she not come in? It was quite dark outside. I ran out, calling, "Delia! Delia!" Then I saw her, huddled against the step, She was dead. Her insides had been torn out, and there was blood on her head.

Why had she not made her usual spring in at the window? Had she left it until too late and become too cold to make the spring, and run round to the door, which did not open, because I was not there to admit her? I looked at my cats. All were on the sofa. There was no blood on them, nor any sign of struggle. They looked peaceful.

I do not think I have ever been more shocked and distracted in my life. I picked Delia up and walked about with her, not knowing what to do. I laid her in the cool grass, then went into the house, knelt and touched with my forehead a holy figure and prayed, "Maitreya, be with her. Tell me what to do for her."

It came to me I had been wrong to lay her outside. She had been trying to get in. She was still warm, and some consciousness perhaps remained in her body. I brought her in again, and laid her on her usual folded newspaper on the sill. "You are home now, Delia. I will shut the window to keep out the draught."

In the morning, when the body was stiff, I carried it to the flower-bed nearest the bathroom window, where I dug a grave. I could find only a brick to lay over the head I loved, "But *she* is in my bosom."

On the 20th, I let the others out for a run, and then went back into the house. Suddenly there was a most terrible screaming and screeching from the garden. I rushed out and saw all my hens being chased by a most extraordinary dog, yellowish-red, with pointed face and prick ears pointing forwards, crouched on low, short legs, on which it made rushes at the birds, its tail drooping behind it in the long grass. Whoever keeps a dog like that? I ran at it, shouting, "Go away! 'way! 'way!" waving my arms, and shepherding the hens into their run. Now I knew what had killed Delia.

It was nowhere to be seen. I was sure it had not gone out of the garden gate, which was, anyway, bolted. It must have run along the top of the stone wall. . . . Only then did it come to me that it must have been a fox.

The only hen not in the enclosure, it was she for whom he had gone. To fly in at the window she had always to crouch for a moment to make the spring; she had not had time and so had run to the door, that did not open. . . . I went to Podington and bought a round, flat decorated stone, with which I replaced the brick. Accidentally I uprooted a violet, and replaced it, saying, "Let only violets grow where Delia lies."

IN MY BOSOM

TIUTTÉ STILL ATE well but I could now feel the nodules on her spine. I read that this was a sign of age, so did not think of her as ill but old. It was only a couple of days before Christmas that I noticed that whereas she had hollows between backbone and hips, she was fuller beneath. On Christmas Eve, this fullness beneath was more pronounced – but my taxi was at the door. Arrived at Tim's, I told him, "Tiutté is not looking right. I'll take her to the vet when I get home."

I got back on the morning of Boxing Day. Bambina and Alexander stood up in the sitting room; Cleo emerged from the study. Outside the hens were clamorous. I fed and watered them; and I looked for Tiutté. I went back into the house, calling, "Tiutté! Tiutté!" I went upstairs. The door of my bedroom was open, and on the floor I found her, stretched out. She was dead.

Though her teeth were clenched, there was still a little warmth in her body, so it must have been that morning she died. As I carried her downstairs and dug her grave, by the big poppy at the west side of Cynthia's, I remembered her pitiful beginnings. "Those people were going to put you down. At least I have given you a life, fifteen years, Tiutté. You are now in my bosom."

I went next day to Podington, and brought back a stone to lay over her. And I wrote and told the Swiss boys.

On the 28th the shop opened again and I went to thank Lesley for having come in to feed my cats and hens. She asked, "Have you got a cat that's pregnant?"

"No, but I know what you saw." I told her that one was dead.

Lesley said, "She was very eager for her food both days. When I went in at breakfast time on Boxing Day she was standing in the kitchen waiting for it. And she couldn't keep away from the milk."

Bambina was now not looking at all well, and I was terrified of her going the same way as her mother. Allan Adams did not open again until the 30th, when I was waiting with Bambina for the door of his surgery to open at 9.00. "Her mother died on Boxing Day and she does not look at all well."

He said Bambina was suffering from severe dehydration and that her liver was slightly enlarged. Dehydration meant kidneys not working well and I thought, now, that Tiutté's swelling was dropsical.

He gave Bambina an injection, prescribed two kinds of pills and vitamin B tablets: I should keep her on low protein foods, fish, chicken, turkey, rabbit, no red meat. (I had, in fact, avoided giving it.)

"She isn't drinking water."

"Is it always available?"

"Yes, but she refuses it and drinks milk."

"All you can do is keep water available all the time."

So we passed into 1988. On 16 February, Bambina again drank water. Next morning after breakfast she drank it again. After that she gave up milk as the first drink of the day and drank water as before.

When Tim came for my birthday on 7 March the three cats stayed. It was the first time Cleo had not fled.

But during April I became increasingly concerned about Bambina. Her coat had become ragged, she looked tired and the fear came to me that I should not have her much longer. Spurred by this, I made another portrait of her, in the window, *contre jour*, and one on the low coffee-table, the lamp-light full on her.

On 23 May, I said to her, "You're going to see Allan Adams again," and packed her into her basket.

He examined her himself, and said, "She has a tumour on the liver."

I was horrified. "Can you perform an operation to remove it?"

He said he would not like to operate without first trying what medicine could do and gave me pills for her. "That's a ten days' course. If after ten days she is no better, I'll operate."

Terribly depressed, I carried her home and gave her the first of the pills; also homeopathic Nat. Sulph. I rang Tim. His reaction was gloomy. "A tumour on the liver is bad news." He wondered even if it would be possible for surgery to get at it.

The next morning, she was sitting as before in the window, looking very ill. Her eyes were nearly closed. I rang Allan Adams. "I'm afraid she will not last ten days. She must have the operation."

He gave me an immediate appointment, and I put her in the basket and drove her over. I had been in a terrible indecision, in case the operation proved fatal, and talked to her all the way. The receptionist took the basket from me, and suddenly I wanted it back from her, for a moment. I said, "May I see her again?" I looked — feeling it could be for the last time — at her through the little window, and said, "I'm not abandoning you, darling. I'm confiding you to the doctor to be made well."

I drove home and sat and meditated for her during the hours that passed while he might be operating. "Morya, may his hand be skilled. May she survive." I called on the seven Masters and those above the Masters. "May she survive and be made well."

I had been told I could fetch her at 4.00 and was there beforehand, dreadfully fearing. The receptionist said, smiling, "No food tonight. And keep her indoors for a few days." These words told me she was alive. I had expected her to be unconscious, but through the little window she was looking out. I drove her home and carried her upstairs before I opened the basket. She looked around, stepped out. The operation must have been skilful for there were no marks on her coat. She walked slowly, a little stiffly, but looked better than she had in the morning.

That night she slept in the upstairs room, as she used to do, and in the morning as I used, I opened the door for her to come into my room before I sat down in lotus, and asked a certain Master, "May the seed of your blessing grow . . . in this little one who is always present at the blessing, participates in the blessing, is blessed."

But then I noticed something red protruding. She must have gnawed through her stitches. I gave her breakfast and took her back to Allan Adams. His young assistant said, "It's a piece of fat. I'll have to put her under again to cut it off." Poor mite, she had little enough fat on her thin body that I was trying to build up. . . . At 4.00, when I collected her, I was told again, "No food tonight."

"It's the second night running."

"She'll last. If she eats, she will be sick."

That night I left open the door of my own room, so that she could join me on my bed. She walked about on me, but it was a dear disturbance of sleep that told me she was alive. At 4.00 a.m. I got up and risked opening the carton of Sheba chicken and turkey I had brought upstairs. She ate it ravenously, and was not sick.

I kept her upstairs all that day and the next, but outside it was sunny and on the 27th, in the late afternoon, I took her down and on to the patio for a short while. She sat on the patio quietly, and I took a photograph, and from it I made a painting, which I called *Bambina, The Thanksgiving Picture.*

On 6 June I took her to have her stitches out, and on the 16th I took her back because one of her eyes was watering. The assistant vet gave me drops for the eyes, but said she had slight gingivitis, inflammation of the gums, caused by tartar on the teeth. "I could easily remove it, but it would mean knocking her out again." I did not want her put under a third time, so he gave me pills to give her.

On 18 June I wrote, "Bambina's eyes seem to be better" and on 11 July, "Bambina so much better it is a joy to see her springing about, jumping from mantelpiece to cabinet across door."

She had never looked in my eyes more graceful. It was strange that she possessed a fineness exceeding that of either of her parents, and remembering something Blavatsky had written in *Isis* about the power of images on the foetus, I murmured to her of the mystery:

> Did my thoughts shape you in your mother's womb
> That you have bones so fine?
> Did I know before the moment came
> The threads were weaving on the loom?
> Did I prepare you to be born?
> Were you fore-destined to this room?

It was my besetting concern she should reach her fourteenth birthday, and as we passed into August I began to feel confident. In the early hours of 22 August I was wakened by Bambina. My clock showed it was 3.50. She was licking me and kneading me for all she was worth, her whole body vibrant with her expression of love. I caressed her and tried to calm her, but she was intoxicated with excitement, turning round on me, kneading and licking. "Bambi darling! Bambi darling. Bambi darling!"

When I rose, a little before my usual time, she was with me in my morning meditation, still rubbing herself against me, but when she went down to join the others and I opened a tin, she hung back, hardly eating. She had suddenly gone very weak. Had her ecstatic behaviour during the night so exhausted her that she now was all in?

I drove her to Allan Adams and told him this story. He said, "She is quite well, but very pale. She is anaemic. That accounts for the sudden flagging." He gave her an injection, and when she had received it she stepped back neatly into the basket to be brought home.

I gave her now the homeopathic remedies for anaemia: Nat.Mur., Ferrum Phos. and Calc Phos. When on 31 August I took her back to Allan Adams for a repeat injection, his assistant, who saw her, said, "She does not look anaemic to me."

On 26 September, I was able to say to her, "Many happy returns" on her fourteenth birthday. In the garden she settled in the long grass, forming, beneath a long and trailing branch of the old Bourbon rose, a perfect picture, and I marvelled that through fourteen years, in despite of all hazards and alarms, I had managed to preserve this tiny parcel of life.

Later, in the white garden chair, she frolicked with Edward.

Three days after her birthday I took her back to Allan Adams for a check up. He saw her himself and said, "She is no longer anaemic." Her gums were a little red, but he agreed she should not be put under again. He found no return of the tumour on her liver, yet, he said, it was a little large. I should continue to restrict her diet to fish and white meats. She stepped back into her basket, in the way that made us smile.

Tim, when he came for his birthday, said, "She looks a lot better than when I saw her last." And he confided to me, "I still dream of Dizzy." Dizzy was his cat.

On 18 October I took her to Allan Adams for a further check up. The assistant vet said, "I'm very pleased with her. She looks very well." She stepped back into her basket.

Cleo began to give me concern. She had become very restive, almost aggressive, clawing at me as I settled for tea or when I did my evening yoga.

20 November brought the first snow. On the 25th there was an interruption to the electricity supply, which caused the central heating to go off. I turned on the gas fire, but that was not the same thing, and Bambina looked chilled. It was a pity, because she had been so well, and this ended the period of her being so. Next morning, however, she ate a normal breakfast, and I wrote, "Thank God." But on the 27th I wrote, "Bambina not eating again this evening." It was a Sunday. Next morning she ate no breakfast and I drove her to Allan Adams, saying, "I think she has a temperature." He took it, and said, "She has a temperature, all right."

He gave her something to bring it down, and as soon as we returned she ate, and the next morning I recorded, "Bambina still eating." But on the 30th I woke to find the central heating had failed in the night. Bambina was chilled and ate no breakfast. I took her back to Allan Adams. He found no temperature this time but gave her an injection and pills to stimulate appetite. I said, "She hasn't got too much flesh on her. I would like to see those little hollows in her flanks filled out."

"That you may never do," he said. "She will not get back that bloom, after the trouble she has had. There will very likely be a recurrence."

Very depressed, I prayed for her. The gas men got the heating working again and on 9 December I wrote, "Bambina well. Went out for 40 minutes tonight and came back leaping through the cat-flap."

On 17 December, however, I was dismayed by her appearance. She had lost fur from the right side of her face between ear and eye, and on right shoulder-blade behind ear. How had it happened? Had she been attacked? I thought more likely she had caught herself on some jagged wire, and after medicating her examined the wire around the gate, turning all ends in. But on the 22nd there was more of her fur missing and she ate no breakfast. I took her to Allan Adams. He drew the curtain to darken the room and passed over her an instrument which emitted a blue light. Then he said, "She has not got ringworm. She has a non-infectious dermatitis." He gave her an injection to bring her temperature down and gave me anti-viral tablets to give her, and also a lotion, Quellada, to allay the irritation that caused the self-destructive scratching. As soon as we got home, she ate.

Later, in the afternoon of the same day, I took Cleo, for a check up before the holiday. The young assistant vet approved her, "She's terrific! For her age!"

I went for Christmas to Tim, and when I got back on Boxing Day wrote, "Found Bambina safe and well and actually better than when I left her." But on the 30th she was scratching at her shoulders, tearing her fur and drawing blood. I immediately applied more of the lotion, and on the 31st, when she started again.

However, my first entry for 1 January, 1989 was, "Bambina better. Skin looks healthy and no longer enflamed." On the 4th I took her back for a check up, and a new assistant vet, a woman, Adrienne Pankhurst, examined her and said, "No medication is needed."

On 11 January, I wrote, "Bambina's sides are filling out," and on the 22nd, "Bambina's hair is really growing again." But on 3 February she was scratching again and I had to take her back to the vet: more tablets to stop the scratching. Then, on 2

March she was drinking water so continually I wondered if it was a symptom of something and drove her back to Allan Adams. "She sits over the bowl all the time."

He said she was well except that her kidneys were beginning to fail, as happened with old cats. My heart sank, for I knew it was of kidney failure that most cats died, and it saddened me to hear her called an old cat. She was still my kitten to me.

Tim, when he came on 7 March, thought she was looking better and less thin. Whilst he sat on the sofa I made a new painting of him; it had to be rapid as we wanted to walk up and see the little oak-tree before he had to go.

On 7 April Bambina was hugging the fire again and I drove her back to Allan Adams'. Mrs. Pankhurst found her liver to be enlarged.

I said she had a major operation on it last year and I did not know if she could stand going under anaesthetic again. Studying her record, Mrs. Pankhurst decided to give her an injection. Bambina stepped back into her basket.

On our return she was better, and next day I wrote, "Bambina eating well."

On 27 April it was Cleo who was not eating and I drove her to Allan Adams'. As Mrs. Pankhurst opened her mouth, her one remaining tooth came out into her hand. "It couldn't have been much use to her, with nothing coming up to meet it." (I had not noticed them go.) "No temperature but her breathing is a little congested." She gave her an injection.

On 4 July I took Bambina back, just for a check. A new assistant vet, Mr. Farnam, confirmed she was well.

It was about 9.00 in the evening of 14 August that I noticed a peculiarity in Cleo's breathing. We were on the sofa, and she was on the arm behind my right shoulder. Her sides were being drawn in, in sudden jerks. I gave her Mag.Phos., the anti-spasmodic, and in the morning drove her to Allan Adams'. I told Mrs. Pankhurst I feared her heart might be irregular. She put a stethoscope to it and said, "Her heart's all right, but there is a lump in her chest."

"Does that mean she has to be operated?"

"No, I'll give her an injection."

Bambina had been spending her days enjoying the sunshine by a clump of irises in the garden, but now began to spend most of her time indoors on top of the refrigerator. I took her back to Allan Adams'. Mrs. Pankhurst said, "She will become more like that. Her liver is very much enlarged."

She agreed with me that there should not be another operation. "I could not guarantee the result. I'll try conservation. If her condition continues to deteriorate, it may be necessary to make a decision."

I was appalled. I would never "make a decision". As I carried her back to the car, I said, "You still have your fifteenth birthday to make . . . if after that you cannot make it longer, it will be in my arms . . . at home . . . in my arms. . . ."

The vitamin injection must have done her some good, for that evening I wrote, "Bambina very much better. Went in and out naturally, and this evening is not on the fridge but sitting on the arm of the sofa. I am giving her Nat.Sulph."

On 24 August I was again sitting on the sofa, with Cleo on my right side, when I noticed her eyes were filled with water, the right half-shut. It was again about 9.00 in the evening. I gave her Nat.Mur. and next morning drove her to Allan Adams'. Mr Farnam said, "Oh dear!" It was conjunctivitis. There was nothing else wrong with her and he handed me a cream which he showed me how to squeeze over her eyes three times a day, to both sooth and counteract the infection.

When I got home with Cleo I could not see Bambina. I searched in every room and in the garden, calling. It was like the old days. Then, in the kitchen, I saw the twitch of an ear. She was in a small cupboard above the formica working surface in which I kept my china. It was to be her new nest. I removed the china from it and lined it with soft cloths.

On Sunday 27 August, despite the cream in her eyes, Cleo looked so peaceful, sitting in the half-open doorway to the garden that I left it so for her while I visited the little oak-tree. She was still there when I came back, and I took what was to be the last photograph.

On Tuesday 29 August, at about 5.30, I was just opening a tin to give the cats their "tea", when, to my horror, I saw that Cleo was dragging herself forward on her belly, unable to stand. She was struggling gamely, full of courage, but even on her belly could no longer keep upright, but fell on her side, though still using her legs in the endeavour to propel herself forward.

The surgery would still be open, but I had taken my car in for a repair. Tony had promised the car back this afternoon, but at what time? Would it be quicker to call a taxi? I telephoned Lewis's and said, "It's an emergency. One of my cats is dying. How quickly can you deliver?"

"In ten minutes," said Christine.

In ten minutes it was at the door. I already had Cleo in the basket and drove her to Allan Adams'. There were a lot of people in the waiting-room and I told the receptionist, "It's an emergency." She took the basket from me and I was shown straight through into a passage where I was left to wait. I was afraid Cleo was already dead or being given a mortal injection, and I called on every holy name I knew to ease her passing. "Be with her in these last moments."

Mr. Farnam came down. "Her heart is failing. She is slipping in and out of consciousness. There is nothing I can do. Except one thing."

Now she lay on the table, curled. Farnam went out of the room for a minute. Cleo looked so far gone I thought she was already dead, for I could see no movement. Confused, I asked the girl, "Has he done it already?"

"No, he has gone to prepare the injection."

Suddenly her toothless mouth opened very wide, and a cry came out. This thing happened again and again, rhythmically. It was with every breath she took that the mouth opened and the cry came out. The cries were not complaints. I did not think she was conscious of emitting them. Her breathing caused them automatically.

Farnam was back, with the injection. He shaved an area of fur from her leg, wiped it with something and inserted the needle.

"This is done in love," I told her. "I love you. You are surrounded by love."

He had to insert the needle several times before all movement ceased. In the silence, I was calling upon the names of all the Masters, asking them to be present, with her, receive her.

"Would you like to take her home, to bury her?" he asked.

"Yes."

I took her back in the basket, still talking to her. "Now you are in my bosom forever. Like Cynthia. Like Tiutté. You are in my bosom forever."

Where should I bury her? It was on the patio, near the pillar, she had liked to sit. Near to the pillar, in the shade of the white buddleia, I dug her grave. As I placed her within it, I said, "You are no longer within the body being lowered. You are within my bosom."

As I returned to the house there was a ring at the door. It was Ken, with a basin filled with apples that had fallen from one of my trees their side of the fence. "Cleo is dead," I told him. "Tell Stella." And I rang Tim, then wrote to the Swiss boys.

In the morning, Stella was at my door. "I'm so sorry about Cleo." I asked her about Little Girl. "She is very thin and it's difficult to know what to give her to eat. She's fourteen and a half now."

I drove to Podington for a stone for Cleo's grave, still talking to her as I laid it.

When I cross the bar, it will be carrying in my arms a cargo of little souls.

On 3 September Bambina came and sat on my lap again, instead of on the top of the fridge. "That's better." Better still, on 5 December, whilst I was typing, she came to the door of my study, and with her tiny, soft miaow, told me it was lunch-time, and fetched me to the kitchen. "You're really going to make it to your fifteenth birthday." And I prayed, "May she make it to her fifteenth birthday."

But she forsook her usual place by the irises for the alley between the raised rose-bed and the house; it was not soft and I could only think she found it more sheltered. On the 18th I wrote, "Bambina seems weak, though she still comes down to eat. Took her out for a few minutes while the sun was out, then she came in." I photographed her almost every day, and carried her upstairs to take, in the mirror, a photograph of her in my arms. (Later I made a painting from this.) I told Tim on the 'phone, "If she makes it to her fifteenth birthday I'll ask for her to make it to yours, so that you will see her again."

"I'd like to see her again."

On 20 September I wrote, "Bambina still well." And on the 21st, "Bambina went out of her own accord and lay in the long grass from about 4.30 to 6.30, probably because it is very hot." On the morning of the 22nd – the fourteenth anniversary of that on which I missed Cynthia – I drew my curtains to see Bambina on the patio. On Saturday 23rd I went in to Rushden to collect my framed painting of roses from Studio 13 and saw a placard advertising fresh fish in the market. There was now no fish-shop or poulterer in Rushden, only chance at the market on Saturdays. Her birthday would be on next Tuesday. I dared not leave it till the Saturday beyond, and bought her, now, fresh fillets of plaice. Only three days to go now. She had made her permanent bed in the china cupboard and each night, when I left her, I said, "May Masters bless and keep you through the night." Each morning when I came down, she rose to greet me, the slender white pillars of her forelegs still apparently firm, and walked along the blue formica top to the spot from which she could descend to the chair and thence to the floor, where she waited with Alexander and Edward while I opened a tin. On 24 September I recorded, "Bambina out again for quite a while." On 25 September I did her birthday shopping: Princes breasts of chicken, Princes salmon and Princes sardines. In the evening she was still well. She lay for a while on a leisure-suit I had taken off, then on the painting I had made of her crossing the lawn by the white buddleia. Then she retired to her cupboard. "You are going to make it. Darling, you have almost made it." I sat up with her until a few minutes to twelve. Then, so that I should be able to speak the traditional words on the morrow, I went upstairs.

On the morning of the 26th when I came down to the kitchen, she was alive and rose to greet me as I said, "Many Happy Returns of the Day, Bambina. You are fifteen today."

She came down. I opened the breasts of chicken and to my relief it was an immense success with her. I photographed her as she ate voraciously. She lapped water from the bowl and went out, and sat on the grass by Cynthia's grave. I could not really believe she knew who lay beneath it, yet it was as if she did; their faces had been like the two halves of one flower. I photographed her, and again, as she turned towards Edward.

In the afternoon I opened the Princes. It was in the afternoon she had been born.

As the perfect birthday ended, I said again, "May Masters bless and keep you through the night."

The next day when I came down she was weaker. I had been asking the Masters — particularly the Master Saint-Germain whom I felt would be closest to cats — to keep on preserving her, but as she walked along the formica top, one of her hind-legs missed its footing — as though it were stiff — and she almost fell.

That night I built up her bed in the cupboard with further soft cloths. "May Masters bless and keep you through the night."

On 28 September, when I came down in the morning I never doubted she would rise to greet me, but she remained lying. At first I thought she was dead, but then she moved a little, I put a bowl of water and a saucer with a little chicken on the formica top where she could reach it from where she lay, and she took a little of each. Then she relapsed. Yet she was softly purring. Then her head dropped. To make her comfortable, I slipped my hand beneath it. She opened her eyes, and gazed into mine for a long time. It was a deep communion. "Is this your last feline incarnation? Or will you come back to me?"

I felt that she had been sustained till her fifteenth birthday because I had asked for it, but could not be sustained longer. I did not expect her to rise again. I prayed, "Saint-Germain, I have asked you each day to preserve her. Now I ask you to take her, to ease her passing."

The purring had stopped. The breathing became jerky. "There is only one place for you to pass away. In my arms," I said, and lifted her from the cupboard and sat with her in the chair by the sitting-room window overlooking the garden.

By 2.00 there was a jerk with every breath. Head and tail jerked. Yet the jerks, which came with every breath, were rhythmic, and she seemed peaceful. I prayed to all the seven Masters of Wisdom, asking them each in turn to ease her passing, bless and keep her. I prayed to those above the Masters of Wisdom. I petitioned the highest.

It was 3.15 when I noticed the jerks had stopped. Her breathing now was very fine and light, spiritual. There was a wonderful atmosphere in the room, so wonderful that I said to her, "All the angels are with you. All the Brothers are with you."

It was 3.19 when I saw she had ceased to breathe.